TWISTED TOYFARE THEATRE

10TH ANNIVERSARY COLLECTION

BY THE STAFF OF
TOYFARE MAGAZINE

AS PUBLISHED BY
WIZARD ENTERTAINMENT

+ editorial

GIVE ME BACK MY ASS!

A guest introduction by writer Jeph Loeb

I love "Twisted ToyFare Theatre"...but I've got a bone to pick with it.

A few years ago the "TTT" guys contacted me and asked me for a quote for the back cover of one of their books. So I said, "'Twisted ToyFare Theatre' is laugh-your-ass-off funny. It fact, I've been reading it so long I don't have an ass."

But that wasn't a joke...that was a cry for help! Now here we are three years later and absolutely no attempts at restitution have been made!

Not having an ass has been traumatic. I now find myself not fitting into most pants, and I blame "Twisted ToyFare Theatre." I blame them and I'm suing, actually. The reason I agreed to do this introduction is because I was hoping it was part of a settlement where I get my ass back.

But despite the ass trauma, I can't stop reading "Twisted ToyFare." There's so much to love. I love it when the Hulk has to go to the bathroom. Which actually happens quite a bit in these pages.

I love knowing that I'm laughing along with all the other major players in the comics industry. I know Geoff Johns gets all the stories that he does for *Justice Society of America* from "Twisted ToyFare Theatre." I know for a fact that the reason why *The Ultimates* is always late is because Mark Millar is always reading "TTT." I know absolutely beyond a shred of a doubt that before "TTT," Brian Michael Bendis had a full head of hair. He read it and it was so good that he pulled his own hair out. Maybe he can join my class-action lawsuit–his hair and my ass.

But I have to say a great deal of my affection for "Twisted ToyFare" is because it was a favorite of my son, Sam. Sam is no longer with us, but when *ToyFare* would come in the mail Sam would always take it, and I could hear him cackling in the other room, almost like he couldn't breathe because he was laughing so hard. So for that reason alone it has a very special place for me. Sam would absolutely make it a highlight of the month.

Sam and I always loved the way the "TTT" creators put bug-eyes on the characters to represent...well, just about every emotion. It looks bad, but it's purposely bad. *Gen*^{13} creator J. Scott Campbell once said to me that what made *Buffy the Vampire Slayer* enjoyable for him was that the women were sexy and the monsters were really goofy and it looked like they had rubber all over them. I think that's the charm of "Twisted ToyFare Theatre." It looks like it's made for three cents, but it gives you about 89 cents worth of fun.

So someone is making a profit, and that profit could be spent in order to get my ass back.

Jeph Loeb has written a lot of stuff. He's a co-executive producer of and a writer on NBC's smash hit Heroes. *He was the supervising producer of and a writer on* Lost *and* Smallville. *He even wrote* Teen Wolf *and* Commando. *Oh, and he's written a ton of acclaimed comic books, including* Batman: The Long Halloween *and the highly anticipated* Ultimates Volume 3. *In lieu of sending Jeph an ass, ToyFare will be donating to the Sam Loeb College Scholarship Fund. To find out how you can donate, email* **samloeb4@aol.com**.

36

TTT 10TH ANNIVERSARY

contents

features

TWISTED TOYFARE THEATRE 10th ANNIVERSARY COLLECTION

Please direct all editorial-related inquiries to Wizard Editorial Dept., 151 Wells Avenue, Congers, NY 10920-2064 (or Fax: 845-268-0053).

ANNOY ALL MONSTERS!

As originally published in *ToyFare* #95

GUYS, *GUYS*, GUESS WHAT *I* JUST DID!

I DUNNO, ATE A GIANT SWEATER?

"Although he had been parodied thousands of times (including in a 'TTT'-style online comic), we thought we could bring something new to the character of Godzilla—namely the idea of this massive lizard being utterly oblivious to the plight of the tiny humans around him. We thought it worked, and apparently the fans did, too.* Unfortunately, Godzilla toys aren't very poseable and we had to cut him into 27 pieces to make him do everything he does in this strip. Hot glue, we love you!"

- Zach Oat, "Twisted ToyFare" Writer

* This strip was chosen as one of the top 25 strips by voters at wizarduniverse.com

Twisted ToyFare Theatre
PRESENTS
ANNOY ALL MONSTERS!
BY: McCALLUM, OAT & ACLIN
WITH: GUTIERREZ, KARDON & WARD
BLOOP...
BLOOP
BLOOP
BLOOP
GRRAAAAAHHHH!

GRAA-AAAWN!
...SMACK SMACK

BLOOP
BLOOP
BLOOP

I *TOTALLY* OVERSLEPT.
GOJIRA! GOJIRA HAS RETURNED!
QUICK! MOBILIZE THE FIGHTER JETS!

MAN, IT FEELS *GOOD* TO STRETCH THE LEGS AFTER ALL THAT HIBERNATING.
RATATATATAT
SMASH!
BOOM!
CRASH!

I WONDER IF THE GUYS ARE-- *GAMERA!*
YO, GAMERA, DOWN *HERE*, MAN!

SO HOW'S IT GO--
HWARLF!
AAAIIEE, IT BURNS!
MY BABY!

YO...IF THAT'S WHAT HAPPENS EVERY TIME YOU SPIN, WHY DON'T YOU JUST WALK?
DUDE, I'M A TURTLE.
YOU HAVE ANY IDEA HOW LONG THAT'D TAKE?
RRRING
READY THE LASER CANNON, IT'S OUR ONLY HOPE!

Y'ELLO...
GAMERA... YOU MUST PICK UP MILK ON THE WAY HOME!
HURRY!

DUDE, I DON'T EVEN PRETEND TO UNDERSTAND THAT RELATIONSHIP.
TWO HOT ASIAN CHICKS WHO DON'T KNOW ABOUT UNDERWEAR?
WHAT'S NOT TO UNDERSTAND?
FIRE!
ZAP!
ZAP!
ZAP!

WHAT THE... MY FOOT JUST FELL ASLEEP.
AW, CRAP... MOTHRA JUST SPOTTED US.
HE'S COMING OVER.
STOMP!
STOMP!
STOMP!
IT'S JUST MAKING HIM ANGRIER!
AIIEEEE...!

GUYS, GUYS, GUESS WHAT I JUST DID!
I DUNNO, ATE A GIANT SWEATER?

...HAR-HAR.
NO, I JUST FOUGHT BIOLANTE!
ISN'T HE JUST A BIG FLOWER?
SOMETIMES.

...
OH, HEY, CHECK IT OUT, THE *SUN!*
THE *BRIGHT, SHINY* SUN...
oooOOOooo...

MUST... TOUCH...THE LIGHT...
FLAP
FLAP
FLAP

FLAP
FLAP
FLAP

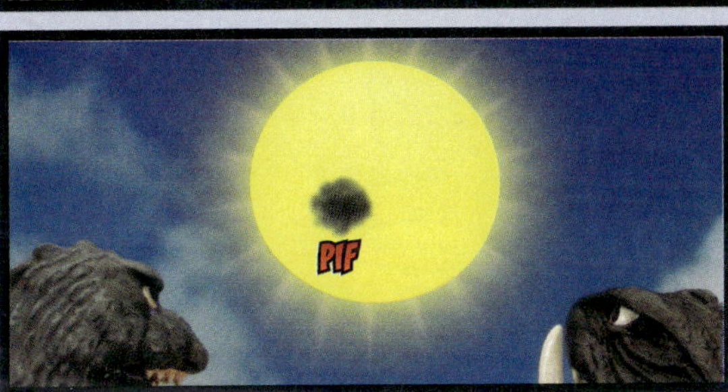
PIF

GIVE *GHIDORA* A CALL, SEE IF HE WANTS TO HANG OUT.
OH, FOR... I'M *ROAMING*.
YOU OWE ME A BEER.

HELLO?
YO, *GHIDORA!*
WHO?
...GHIDORA?
I'M SORRY, *WHO?*
SIGH
'KING' GHIDORA.

SPEAKING.
YEAH, 'ZILLA AND ME ARE HANGIN' OUT AND WANTED TO KNOW IF--
BEEP!
HOLD ON, I'VE GOT ANOTHER CALL...

HEY, *GAMERA!*
...GHIDORA?
HANG ON, I'LL GET HIM.

HELLO...?
YO!
YOU'VE GOT KING GHIDORA.
CLICK
OY.

YES?
...HELLO?
YOU'VE GOT KING GHIDORA...

HOW'S HIS MAJESTY?
THE SAME.
HEY, YOU THINK THOSE HEADS EVER MAKE OUT?
UNLEASH PROJECT X-16!
MAY GOD HELP US!

YOU MEAN WITH EACH OTHER, OR WITH OTHER PEOPLE?
EITHER. I CAN'T REMEMBER THE LAST TIME GHIDORA GOT LAI--
WHAT THE HELL IS THAT THING?!?

THAT'S *AWESOME!*
IT'S LIKE A ROBOT *ME!*
THANKS MAN, YOU *SHOULDN'T* HAVE.
DUDE, IT *WASN'T* ME.
MECHA-GOJIRA, ATTACK ALPHA NOW!

GAH!
IT'S PISSING MISSILES!
WHERE'S THE REMOTE?
FWOOSH!
BOOM!
BLAM!
KA-POW!
I DON'T KNOW, I JUST GOT IT!
IT'S WORKING!
WE'RE SAVED!

YOU'RE THE ONE WITH THE SHELL! CONTROL-ALT-DELETE HIM OR SOMETHING!
I'M ON IT!
THOOM!
BAM!

LET'S SEE... IF I DIAL DOWN THE CENTER...
BOOP
BEEP
BOP

WHOA, HEY, WHAT'D I DO?
FWOOSH!
NO, MECHA GOJIRA!
COME BACK!

WHIZZZ!
AW, MAN... THAT THING LOOKED EXPENSIVE.
SORRY, DUDE.
MAYBE WE CAN GO TO SHARPER IMAGE AND GET YOU A NEW ONE.
BOOM!
RING!

HELLO? OH, UH, YEAH, I'M LEAVING NOW.
YES, YES, I'LL PICK UP THE MILK.
I LOVE YOU, TOO.
ALL HOPE IS LOST!
PREPARE FOR THE MASS SUICIDE!

WA-*PISH!*
WA-*PISH!*
YOU ARE *SO* WHIPPED.
SORRY, I CAN'T HEAR YOU... I'M FLYING HOME TO *GET SOME*.
LATER.
MASS SUICIDE IN THREE... TWO...

WELL, THAT WAS A TOTAL WASTE.
WAIT!
HE...HE'S LEAVING!

WE'RE SAVED!
WE'RE...
...WAIT...
HE'S COMING BACK!

WHAT'S GOING ON?
WHAT'S HE DOING?

KER-SPLASH!
RUMMMMMBLE
...OH NO...

BLOOP
BLOOP
BLOOP
THE END?

¡Viva Mego!

As originally published in *ToyFare* #33

"My biggest regret with this strip isn't the insensitivity bordering on racism. Nope, it's the lime-green highlighter I used to color in that Ricky Martin dollar bill. Oh, well, it was a parallel reality. Oh, and check out that early Silver Surfer—just a Thor figure spray-painted silver. And I made that surfboard in approximately eight seconds."

- Tom Root, Former "Twisted ToyFare" Writer, Current *Robot Chicken* Writer/Producer

¡VIVA MEGO!

By Pat McCallum, Tom Root and Douglas Goldstein

All photos by Paul Schiraldi.

NOW TO SET THE FLUX CAPACITOR...
TIK TIK BOOP

AND AS MY TIME PLATFORM HUMS TO LIFE...
...I SHALL ATTACK MEGOVILLE AT ITS MOST VULNERABLE...
VVVVMMMMMMMMMMM...

...1952!
HYUK!
CRACK YER NUTS, GUV'NER?
STEADY, MEN--HE LOOKS... *ARTICULATED* SOMEHOW...
SARGE, MY GUN IS FULL OF PLASTIC!
MUH...MINE TOO!

NYH-HUH! ARE YOU A BOY DOLL OR A GIRL DOLL?
THIS IS GOING TO BE EASIER THAN I THOUGHT.

THESE ANTIQUATED TOYS WILL POSE LITTLE RESISTANCE!
ONCE I DEFEAT THE PAST, *THE FUTURE BELONGS TO DOOM!*

SIXTY SECONDS LATER...
WITH MY ENEMIES DISPATCHED AS IF THEY WERE CHILDREN'S PLAYTHINGS...*
...DOOM STANDS TRIUMPHANT!
THERE... THERE IS NO GOD! ONLY DARKNESS...DARKNESS AND OBLIVION...
...EARN...THISsss...
*THEY WERE CHILDREN'S PLAYTHINGS.

NOW, TO RETURN TO THE TOYLESS MEGOVILLE OF THE PRESENT...
...A RETURN... TO VICTORY!
VVVVMMMMMMMMMM...

SHORTLY, IN THE PRESENT DAY...
NOW, TO-- EH?
COMO SE TACO LA CHIMICHANGA.*
SI.**
*HE WEARS A SKIRT. IF HE DROPS A SOAP, LEAVE IT BE.
**AYE.

ADONDE ESTA EL PESCADO, BURRITO, BURRITO, BURRITO?*
*WE ARE OFF TO THE BEACH TO PLAY LOUD MUSIC.

ZAPATOS CON TITO PUENTE.*
...WORDS FAIL DOOM.
*HERE. BUY A MUSTACHE.

WHAT HAS DOOM WROUGHT?
BY DESTROYING THE PLAYTHINGS OF THE PAST, DOOM HAS CREATED A VOID FILLED BY CHEAP MEXICAN KNOCKOFF TOYS!

WELL, WELL...WHAT DO WE HAVE HERE, PONCH?
LOOKS LIKE TROUBLE, PONCH.
...IT BE A WORLD GONE MAD.

WATCH THE SASS-TALK, GRINGO!
NOW MOVE ALONG--THIS IS NO PLACE FOR A SIESTA!

LATER...
THIS MADNESS MUST END. EVEN DOOM CANNOT FIX IT ALONE. I MUST ENLIST THE AID OF...
'ELLO, OLD BEAN! FANCY A CHALUPA?

...DOCTOR REED RI--
BAXTER CABANA
...NO.

INSIDE...
SU-SAN, I'M HOOO-OOOME!
OH REEDY, BUY ME A LOW-RIDER!
SIIIII!
ONDELAY, ONDELAY, ARIBA!

SUDDENLY...
...IF ONLY DOOM HAD A CAMERA.
SUCH CURIOUS ATTIRE...WHAT DO YOU MAKE OF THIS, *H.O.M.B.R.E.?*
ES BUENO.

MUCH AS DOOM HATES TO ADMIT IT, YOUR ASSISTANCE IS NEEDED. DOOM TAMPERED WITH THE PAST, RESULTING IN THIS MEXICAN ALTERNATE REALITY.

THAT WOULD EXPLAIN THIS MUSTACHE!
THE ANSWER IS OBVIOUS. YOU HAVE TO GO BACK IN TIME AND STOP YOUR PAST SELF BEFORE--*UH*...

ARE YOU OKAY?
DOOM REQUIRES A MOMENT. DOOM...DRANK THE WATER.
HOMBRES

HOURS LATER, IN THE PAST...
...DEVICE THAT WILL MAKE DOOM *MASTER OF ALL MEN!*
VVVVMMMMMMMMMM...

DOOM IS IN TIME!
CONFOUND IT, SURFER, DOOM TOLD YOU-- *THE HELL?*

BLAME RICHARDS.
BLAM!
RICHAR--

SUCCESS! WITH DOOM'S PAST SELF ELIMINATED, HIS CURRENT SELF SHALL... SHALL...
HEY, WAIT A MINUTE.
POP

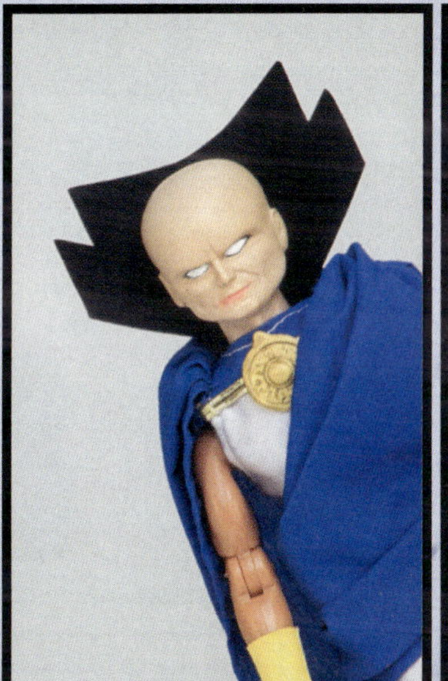

GREETINGS. I AM THE WATCHER!
AND I HAVE BAD NEWS.
UNLIKE THE 'TERMINATOR' FILMS AND HALF OF ALL MARVEL COMICS, YOU CANNOT CHANGE THE PAST.

DOOM'S TAMPERING HAS ENDED ALL REALITY AS YOU KNEW IT, SO...WHAT THE--?
PIÑATA!!
ES BUENO!
AAIIEE!

YO QUIERO TACO BELL!!!
THE END

THE WATCHER

Height: 8.25 inches
Weight: 2.8 oz.
Real Name: Uatu
Occupation: What, are you kidding? His name's not "the Listener," now is it?
Headquarters: Some Moon
First Appearance: "Viva Mego," *ToyFare* #33
Died: "Viva Mego!" *ToyFare* #33
Died: "I Am Legend, Part One," *ToyFare* #84
History: Omniscient foreshadower, or pervy voyeur? Uatu the Watcher rarely falls into the first category when he puts his talents to use. When not gazing upon Kang the Conqueror in the bathroom (*ToyFare* #117), he's peering down on gamblers as head of casino security (*ToyFare* #37) or spying on his neighbor, Dr. Doom (*ToyFare* #38), with high-powered binoculars. His oath "not to interfere with Earthly events" usually lasts about as long as R. Kelly's oath to never pee on women again. On one occasion, he stuck his oversized space-melon into things and warned of Earth's destruction in "Uatu Be in Pictures" (*ToyFare* #44)...only to end up saving the day himself. Yes, Galactus retreated in laughter at the sight of the Watcher's hairless, naked body when Thing de-frocked him from behind. Uatu occasionally uses his power for evil by endlessly voting for Clay Aiken on *American Idol* (*ToyFare* #75) or showing readers a nightmarish planet where children are forced to bear gifts to an all-powerful Santa Claus (*ToyFare* #89).

When he's not "all up in Megoville's grill" about their ill-fated future, Uatu makes ends meet by slumming it as "the Weight Watcher"—a side-show carny who asks people to guess the weight of a stuffed panda (*ToyFare* #62). It was only after Uatu was beaten to death by Mexican children with large sticks (*ToyFare* #33) that it was revealed the Watcher's head is actually filled with delicious hard candy.
Worst Job: Working at the Gap (*ToyFare* #44) and being sworn not to interfere when customers buy "relaxed dobby khakis."

TOYFARE #44 "Uatu Be in Pictures"

TOYFARE #75 "Crisis on Infinite Megovilles"

Bad to be Good

As originally published in *ToyFare* #39

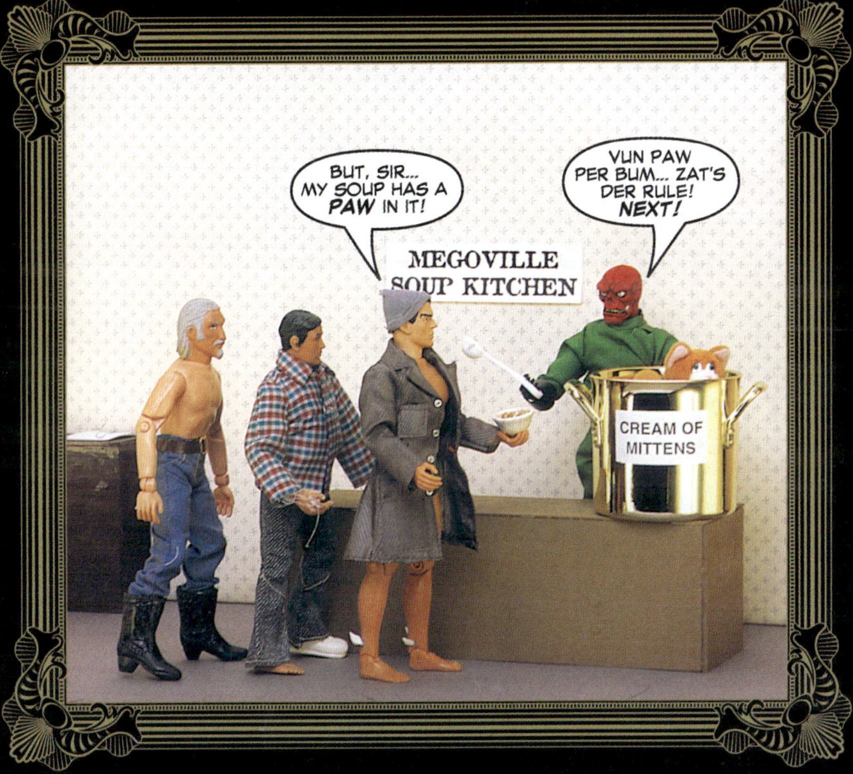

"If you have a premise that fits a large amount of characters, you can have a sketch that's just a series of individual jokes for these characters. We were simply coming up with as many funny ways villains could mess up trying to be good as possible. And it worked. Although I think it was the beginning of a period where we kinda relied on that structure too heavily."

- Doug Goldstein, Former "Twisted ToyFare" Writer, Current *Robot Chicken* Writer/Producer

By Pat McCallum, Tom Root and Douglas Goldstein

SUDDENLY...
WHAT THE--?
IT'SSS HIM!
HIM WHO?

COWER, MORTALS! COWER BEFORE YOUR DARK LORD AND MASTER-- MEPHISTO!

CHEESE IT WITH THE SPECIAL EFFECTS... LARRY DOESN'T WANT US SMOKING DOWN HERE!

SILENCE! I BRING YOU BUT A WARNING... YOUR CURRENT PATHS WILL LEAD YOU ONLY TO MY DOMAIN... THAT OF HELL.
I TELL YOU ONLY OUT OF PROFESSIONAL COURTESY.
UND HOW KIN VE AVOID ZIS FATE?

CHANGE YOUR EVIL WAYS, COMRADES...OR BURN FOR ETERNITY!

BUT...BUT MY PARENTS WERE ATHEISTS!
STOP YOUR SNIVELING, KANG! WE MUST SEIZE THIS FORTUNE AND ACT UPON IT!
HEY... WHERE'S MY SANDWICH?

SOON, IN MANHATTAN...
HELL? NEIN! DER RED SKULL SHALL REMEDY ZIS FATE!

DER STRAYS... DER BUMS...SUCH MISERY!
PERHAPS BOTH SOCIAL BLIGHTS COULD BE CURED... TOGETHER!

BUT, SIR... MY SOUP HAS A PAW IN IT!
VUN PAW PER BUM...ZAT'S DER RULE! NEXT!
MEGOVILLE SOUP KITCHEN
CREAM OF MITTENS

IN ALABAMA...
HOWDY, MR. DOOM! WE SURE DO APPRECIATE YOUR HARD WORK HERE AT HABITAT FOR HUMANITY!
WHO DARES--? OH, IT'S YOU, JIMMY CARTER.

I'M NOT SURE TH' JOHNSON FAMILY NEEDS THIS HERE MOAT, THOUGH, Y'KNOW?
IT'S HIGH TIME THE JOHNSON FAMILY LEARNED THAT THE BEST DEFENSE IS A FORMIDABLE OFFENSE!
GRAWWL!

IN CHICAGO...
HEY! OLD LADY! LET ME HELP YOU THERE!
OH, GOODNESS!

SUCH A CONSIDERATE--AND, UM, PURPLE--YOUNG MAN YOU ARE!
YES! NOT AT ALL LIKE THE KIND OF PERSON WHO WOULD GO TO HELL, RIGHT?

KA-BAM!!
OH, GEEZ.

EUREKA! I CAN ACTUALLY USE MY TIME TRAVEL ABILITY FOR GOOD AND FIX THIS MESS!

FIVE MINUTES AGO...
HEY! BE CAREFUL NOT TO--
EH--?

YOU IMBECILE!
EUREKA! I CAN ACTUALLY USE MY TIME TRAVEL ABILITY FOR GOOD AND--

EVENTUALLY...
I'LL DO IT!
WOULD YOU JUST BACK OFF?
GUYS! WOULD YOU PLEASE JUST LET ME DO THIS?
GOOD HEAVENS!

KA-BAM!!
4x4
Sport Truck

THAT'S...THAT'S REALLY NOT GOOD.

MEANWHILE, AT MICROSOFT'S CORPORATE HEADQUARTERS...
-SIGH- GOOD MOTHER OF GOD, I'M RICH.
-BREEP- MR. GATES, THERE'S A LAWYER HERE TO SEE YOU!

A LAWYER, EH? WHAT DO YOU WANT?
I'M BILL GATES, AND THEREFORE QUITE BUSY!
WELL, SINCE THE MICROSOFT BREAKUP IS TAKING FOREVER, I THOUGHT I'D HELP SPEED THINGS ALONG!

POINK!

HEH HEH! CONSIDER THIS MONOPOLY BUSTED!

POWER TO THE PEOPLE!

"PUNISHER WAR JOURNAL: CAUGHT THE NEFARIOUS GREEN GOBLIN POSING AS A SANITATION WORKER... THE FIEND!"
HMM...AFTER THIS, MAYBE I'LL CLEAN THAT PLAYGROUND ACROSS THE STREET!

THIS ONE'S FOR JUSTICE, PUNK!
BLAM!

AND SO...
...I GAVE THE HANDICAPPED CHILDREN MOONSHINE FOR FREE! HOW'D YOU DO?
I KILLED BILL GATES. WANT A HO-HO?
HEY, IT'S MEPHISSSSSSSS--
YEAH, WE GOT IT, REPTILE. ENOUGH.

I JUST WANTED TO LET YOU GUYS KNOW YOU COULD STOP WORRYING. HELL'S BEEN BOUGHT OUT!
I'M OFF TO KEY WEST!
MICROSOFT
STOCK OPTION

HELL...
DID YOU SEE "FAMILY MATTERS" LAST NIGHT?
THAT SHOW IS ALWAYS ON DOWN HERE.
EXCUSE ME, OH EXALTED ONE, BUT...UM...THE SERVER'S DOWN AGAIN.
PERFECT! IT APPEARS "WINDOWS 2001" IS READY FOR SHIPPING!
END

MEPHISTO

Height: 8 inches
Weight: 3.5 oz.
First Appearance: "Crappy New Year," *ToyFare* #31
Died: "Crappy New Year," *ToyFare* #31
Died: "Viva Mego!" *ToyFare* #33
Died: "If This Be My Roast!" *ToyFare* #83
Died: "I Am Legend, Part One," *ToyFare* #84
History: He may look like the result of Rob Zombie and Tickle Me Elmo's forbidden love tryst, but Mephisto's brand of fuzzy pink evil rules the Megoville underworld. Mephisto goes by many names—the Prince of Lies, the Lord of Hell, Barry—but only one name best describes him: "kind of a jerk." He ruins Y2K celebrations in Megoville Times Square by trying to usher in the Apocalypse (*ToyFare* #31) and even slips Dr. Doom's dead and decomposed mother the tongue while claiming he now "owns her soul and her jammin' booty" (*ToyFare* #83). Occasionally, the Dark God of Hell shows his philanthropic side by hosting *Magic: the Gathering* tournaments for local youth (*ToyFare* #48) and giving X-Men leader Cyclops the ability to "Do the Hustle" in exchange for his immortal soul (*ToyFare* #49). But after giving the keys to hell to Bill Gates in exchange for Microsoft stock options (*ToyFare* #39), Mephisto's days of eternally damning the likes of Daisy Duke (*ToyFare* #53) may be behind him. Nowadays, you're much more likely to find him "slamming a Mountain Dew" wide-mouth can and doing a skateboard hand plant (*ToyFare* #67).
Often Confused with: Dormammu, from the Dark Dimension. Tell them apart with this rhyme: "If the head is afire, Dormammu you desire. If he's super pissed-O, it's Mephisto." See? Easy.

TOYFARE #53 "Redneck Rhapsody"

TOYFARE #83 "If This Be My Roast!"

That '70s Twisted ToyFare Theatre

As originally published in *ToyFare* #49

"The ending was a huge controversy internally. One of the best moments in 'Twisted ToyFare Theatre' history, but it was felt to be too dark by some. We had to bring in the president of the company, because we were deadlocked. The writers said, 'We won't change it, we don't agree with you.' Our magazine department people—who were properly doing their jobs—said, 'Well we think this jeopardizes our sales.' In the end it stayed as is."

- Doug Goldstein

Twisted ToyFare Theatre

presents

BY PAT McCALLUM, TOM ROOT, DOUG GOLDSTEIN AND BILL JENSEN

Photos by Paul Schiraldi.

HEY MAN, YOU MUST BE THAT NEW EXCHANGE STUDENT!
I AM DER SWINGING CAT KNOWN AS DER RED SKULL!
BUT ENOUGH PLEASANTRIES, YA? VERE IS DAT UNCOOL SQUARE CAPTAIN AMERICA, FOR I SHOULD LIKE TO KILL HIM NOW?

THE ARCTIC...
IMPERIOUS REX, MAN!

BAH! VELL, DERE IS ALWAYS PINBALL AT DER STUDENT UNION...
YEESH... I WONDER WHO WE TRADED FOR HIM?

GERMANY...
MY GENITALSSS RETRACT INTO MY ABDOMEN.
NEIN!

ALL RIGHT, TEEN KANG, IF YOU HAVE ANY HOPE OF WINNING THE DANCE CONTEST, YOU'VE GOTTA PRACTICE!
...WHO ARE YOU AGAIN?
FOOLS!
IT SHALL BE TEEN DOOM WHO WINS THE DANCE CONTEST THAT SHATTERS THE FANTASTIC FOUR!

KNOCK! KNOCK!

CHEESE IT, YOU GUYS, I'M TRYING TO STUDY!

TIME FOR THAT LATER!
LISTEN TO FUTURE DOOM, TEEN DOOM! YOU AND DOOM SHALL WORK IN CONCERT TO SMITE DOOM'S ENEMIES WITH--
UM, MY NAME IS VICTOR. AND IT'S REALLY CREEPY TALKING IN THE THIRD PERSON LIKE THAT.
AND WHAT'S WITH YOUR FACE?

SILENCE, TEEN DOOM! SHOW YOUR ELDERS THE RESPECT THEY DESERVE!
GAK! GAAAAK! GAAA--
KRACK!

UMMM...

POP!

AT THE DANCE CONTEST...
OH MAN, I DON'T KNOW. I'M A LITTLE NERVOUS...
OH, STOP BEING SUCH A WUSS!

AH, AH, AH, AH, STAYIN' ALIVE, STAYIN' ALIVE...
HELLO, I AM C-3PO AND THIS IS R2-D2.
WE'RE TOYS FROM THE UPCOMING MOVIE 'STAR WARS' AND WOULD LIKE TO--
TOYS? WHO'S GONNA BUY TOYS LIKE YOU WHEN THEY CAN BUY MEGOS LIKE US?
BEEP-BOOP!

MAN... I'D GIVE ANYTHING TO BE ABLE TO DANCE LIKE THAT...

DID YOU SAY 'ANYTHING'?
ER...
PAFF!

STAYIN' ALIVE, STAYIN' ALIVE...
I'M REALLY DOING IT! I BET I CAN WIN!
I'VE DISCOVERED THE MATHEMATICAL EQUATION FOR GETTIN' YOUR GROOVE ON!

WHO THE... CHUCK XAVIER?
ONE SIDE, KIDS! THE CHUCKSTER LOVES TWO THINGS IN LIFE: THIS HAIR AND DANCING!
UH-OH.

...JUNGLE BOOGIE...OOH! AHH!...JUNGLE BOOGIE...G-G-G-GET DOWN!...
...
SLAP! SLAP!
...JUNGLE BOOGIE...OOH! AHH!...JUNGLE BOOGIE...G-G-G-GET DOWN!...
WOULDJA LOOKIT THAT.
SO...SO GRACEFUL...!
...JUNGLE BOOGIE...OOH! AHH!...JUNGLE BOOGIE...G-G-G-GET DOWN!...
I'D KILL A PUPPY FOR A SIX-PACK.
YEAH!

CRAP IN A HAT!
OH REED! ≶GIGGLE≷ YOU LOST WITH SUCH DIGNITY!
YOU KNOW IT, BABY! SAY, HOW DO YOU FEEL ABOUT ROCKETS WITH POOR PROTECTION?
AW MAN...
IDIOT. I TOLD YOU TO PUT MORE MOTION IN THE OCEAN!
I WON! I WON! THIS IS THE GREATEST DAY OF MY LIFE!

...GREATEST DAY OF MY LIFE...
...GREATEST DAY OF MY LIFE...
...GREATEST DAY OF MY LIFE...
NOOOOOOO!!

...

click

BLAM!
END

THE INVISIBLE WOMAN

Height: 8 inches
Weight: 1.9 oz.
Real Name: Susan Storm-Richards
Group Affiliations: The Fantastic Four, the Secret Avengers, the Mile-High Club
Known Associates: Namor, Luke Cage, the Falcon, Mr. T, Johnny Storm (Adopted brother), Giganto, numerous others
First Appearance: "Blinded by Science," *ToyFare* #17
Died: "X-Mas, Bloody X-Mas," *ToyFare* #30
Died: "Viva Mego!" *ToyFare* #33
Died: "I Am Legend, Part One," *ToyFare* #84
History: Susan Richards is...well, how do we put this politely? The correct term is probably "loose," and we ain't talking about the Mego joints. Although those are also loose.

During her time in the strip, Sue has gone from ditzy, naïve beginnings (*ToyFare* #17) to embracing her filthy, filthy inner-slut. The Invisible Woman relentlessly cheats on her husband, Reed "Mr. Fantastic" Richards. Her sexual exploits extend to a rendezvous with Falcon on the Avengers' Quinjet (*ToyFare* #57), breaking Jenna Jameson's multiple-partner record in front of her own son (*ToyFare* #67), and an invisible, naked slap-and-tickle fight with the Marvel Legends version of herself (*ToyFare* #84).

Known to pop into a scene whenever someone utters the word "skank" (*ToyFare* #73).
Other Talents: Sue engages in many innocent hobbies, including building glass-bottomed boats, churning butter, digging for clams in low tide, laying carpet in the Baxter Building and providing a little mud for Namor's turtle.

HELLO, BOYS...HAVE A GOOD TIME?
I KNOW *I* DID.
WHY'RE THE WALLS COVERED IN *JELLYFISH?*

***TOYFARE* #63** "Variations on a Theme Park"

WELL, JUST BETWEEN YOU AND ME, GET A FEW DRINKS IN MY WIFE AND SHE'S A LITTLE MORE *'OPEN,'* KNOW WHATIMSAYIN'?
YES *SIR*, SOMEBODY'S GETTIN' LUCKY TO-*NITE!*

***TOYFARE* #100** "Someone On This Cover Dies"

The Hunt for Red-Ork-Tober

As originally published in *ToyFare* #62

"Originally, the hunt was for Snarf, but questions over his ownership led us to choose a less problematic but equally annoying sidekick. This strip also has two of our traditional 'let's make fun of our own terrible photography' jokes—namely the fishing pole and sugar cookies. I know they're kind of easy, but I love those jokes. I don't think the strip would be as funny if we took ourselves too seriously."

- Jon Gutierrez, "Twisted ToyFare" Writer

THE HUNT FOR RED ORK-TOBER

BY:
McCALLUM,
ROOT
& OAT

WITH:
BRICKEN,
PATYK,
GUTIERREZ
& ACLIN

EDITORS:
SENREICH &
GOLDSTEIN

AT THAT MOMENT...
OH, BOY! THIS IS GONNA BE THE BEST VISIONARIES PICNIC EVER!
I 'ENVISION' US HAVING A GOOD TIME!
GIGGLE!

POLE POSITION!
THOOM!
SMISH!

I STILL DON'T GET HOW THIS HUNTING TRIP IS FREE.
ALL TAKEN CARE OF BY SOMETHING CALLED THE "AVENGERS CREDIT CARD."
I...I CAN SEE HOLOGRAM GOD!

THAT'S THE BEST PART OF BEING "EARTH'S MIGHTIEST HEROES"...FREE STUFF OUT THE ASS!
THAT AND, UH, HELPING PEOPLE.

SHORTLY...
SO WHO RUNS THIS--
HEY, LIL' HE-MAN DUDE!
SPY-DOR MAN!
...AND YOU KNOW SHIRTLESS SKULL-HEAD GUY HOW?*
DAVE SKELETOR
*"FEAR AND LOATHING IN ETERNIA," TOYFARE #46.

AFTER SPY-DOR MAN HELPED ME KILL HE-MAN, THINGS IN ETERNIA KINDA WENT DOWNHILL.
FIRST HORDAK MOVED IN, THEN WE WERE ALL REPACKAGED AS "HE-MAN IN SPACE," SO I SPLIT BEFORE WE BECAME "HE-MAN BABIES" AND OPENED THIS GAME RESERVE.

AND SO...
SO WHADDYA HAVE IN STOCK FOR OUR HUNT?
WE HAD SOME GREAT *MONCHICHIS* IN YESTERDAY, BUT THE *COWBOYS OF MOO MESA* CLEANED US OUT.
BUT WE DID GET SOMETHING SPECIAL IN JUST THIS MORNING...
SMURF JERKY
NOW WITH 20% LESS HAIR!
FREE!
BATTLE BEAST BITS
WITH EVERY PURCHASE

YOU'RE ABOUT TO LIVE OUT THE FANTASY OF EVERYONE WHO WATCHED CARTOONS IN 1984.
HAIL MARY, FULL OF GRACE, THE LORD IS WITH THEE...

LOCK AND LOAD!
EEEEEEEEEE!

I HATE THAT THING WORSE THAN SNARF.
THE 'O' ON HIS CHEST IS LIKE A TARGET FROM GOD.

JEEZ, HE'S *FAST* FOR A LITTLE GUY WITH NO LEGS.
HEYA FRANK.
LOOKING FOR THE BOBCATS WHO KILLED YOUR FAMILY?
QUIET.
QUACK! QUACK!

TWEET?
GOTCHA!
BUDDA!
BUDDA!
BUDDA!
BUDDA!
BUDDA!

WOO, DOGGIE!
...LET'S GO BEFORE HE CLEANS IT.
I EATS TONIGHT!
...END MY SHAME...
PLOP!

MAN OH MAN!
NOTHING BEATS FISHING! JUST A BOY, NATURE AND HIS SUGGESTIVELY PLACED POLE!
LORDY, I NEED TO GET ME SOME.

WANNA SEE A NEAT TRICK THAT MADE NAMOR INCONTINENT?
HEY, C'MON, I WAS HERE FIRST!
SSSSSS

ZZZIP!
BLORSH!

BWOOP
BWOOP
BWOOP

I'LL BE SEEING THOSE DEAD LITTLE EYES COMING FOR ME IN MY SLEEP...
MAN, ARE THE REST OF THE TEEN TITANS ALL LITTLE MARYS TOO?
CHEESE IT, GUYS. IT'S SPACE TONTO.
AH'M MARSHAL BRAVESTARR, AND YOU'D BEST LISTEN UP.

A-SUMTHIN'S IN THESE A-HERE WOODS, BOYS... T'AINT SAFE!
YOUR WHAT ISN'T SAFE?!?

HEY... GIANT SUGAR COOKIES!
TARNATION!
THOSE'RE ANIMAL TRACKS!

NWARGH?
A CARE BEAR?!?
SHOOT, THAT AINT NO BIG--

GROK!
SLASH!

MRAWHHHH!
AAAAAAHHH!

AWWWW...!

GRAH!
AIIIEEEE!

IMPERIUS REX!
DWEE...?
STAB!

THE POWER OF GRAYSKULL COMPELS YOU!
THE POWER OF GRAYSKULL COMPELS YOU!
SLICE! STAB! POKE!
MUUUUUR...

WOW, I THINK WE ALL LEARNED A VALUABLE LESSON HERE TODAY...
A LESSON WHERE WE ALL LEARNED TO CALL EACH OTHER 'FRIEND.'

LATER...
GREAT BOUTROS BOUTROS-GHALI!
SOMEONE'S CHARGED OVER $7,000 TO A PLACE CALLED 'THE BUNNY RANCH!'
I'LL TAKE THE QUINJET AND CHECK IT OUT.
END

HAWKEYE

Height: 7.75 inches
Weight: 2.3 oz.
Favorite Color: Purple...no, blue!
Group Affiliation: Avengers, National Rifle Association
First Appearance: "Iron Resolve," *ToyFare* #7
Died: "'Til Death Do You Part," *ToyFare* #57
Died: "I Am Legend, Part One," *ToyFare* #84
History: Hawkeye is a master archer and joined the mighty Avengers primarily because it was better than working at the circus. His duties mostly involved looking at a monitor screen and running up a lot of expenses. However, he didn't appear in many early strips because his action figure was owned by someone else, and because he was laying low after murdering another well-known archer (*ToyFare* #18). He eventually cleared his name and joined the cast full-time—just in time to participate in the Secret Wars, where yet another archery contest ended in tragedy as Bo Duke's arms were blown clean off by a dynamite arrow (*ToyFare* #60). Later, Hawkeye went on several other adventures that ended in tragedy: an Orko hunt that ended with Orko, a Care Bear and several Snorks dead (*ToyFare* #62), and his tryout for "Ultimate Idol" where he blew up Bucky (*ToyFare* #67). Most recently, he used a scotch arrow to knock a sober, power-mad Iron Man back off the wagon and put an end to the prohibition-triggered Civil War (*ToyFare* #119). However, while the relapse of an alcoholic would normally be considered a tragedy, most people were willing to let this one slide.
Powers and Abilities: Hawkeye is an above-average archer with a wide range of trick arrows. He also has the keys to the Quinjet and an Avengers credit card with no limit.

TOYFARE #67 "Idol Hands"

TOYFARE #119 "Clean and Super Part 2"

KIRKS UP, HO'S DOWN

As originally published in *ToyFare* #112

"Kirk is one of the few non-superheroes who can hold his own in 'TTT'–the fact that he's one of the original Mego toys helps, but he's always been larger-than-life. The *Next Generation* crew, however, seemed far too boring to do much of anything. When we struck upon the idea of putting the tornado that is Kirk into the stuffy world of Picard and the *Enterprise-D*, we knew we had a way to make it work."

- Zach Oat

BY:
McCALLUM,
OAT &
ACLIN

WITH:
GUTIERREZ
& WARD

SPECIAL THANKS TO:
ARBONA,
COLLINS &
PURDIN

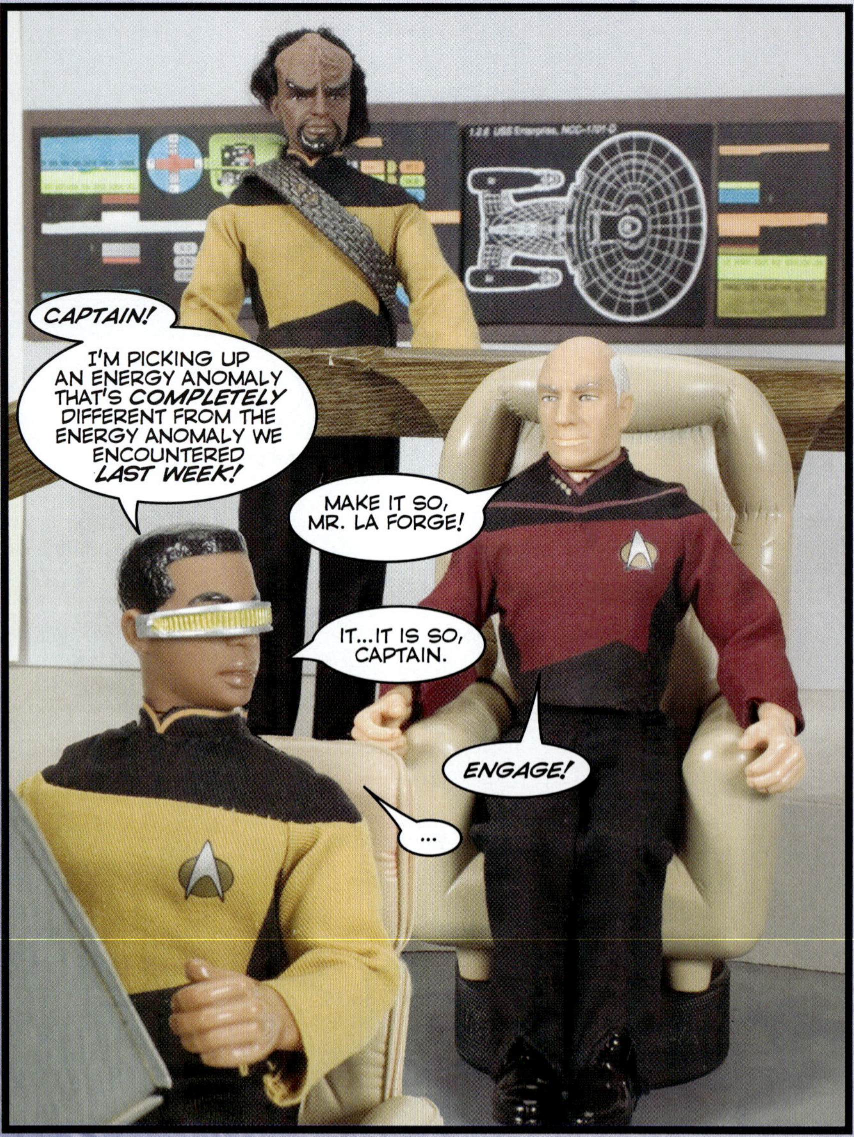

PROFESSOR X!
PHOENIX!
BLACK CYCLOPS!
WHAT ARE YOU DOING HERE IN THE FUTURE?
ER...ACTUALLY, THIS IS THE FUTURE FUTURE. I'M CAPTAIN PICARD OF THE ENTERPRISE D.
WHAT HAPPENED TO YOU?

"I WAS PREPARING TO BEAM DOWN TO BROTHELON-8 WHEN SUDDENLY..."
CAP'N, I...I DINNA EFEEL SO--
HWARLF!
AH, SHI--
VNNN...

...AND NOW I'M HERE.
ANYWAY, I SEE THEY STILL HAVEN'T INVENTED A CURE FOR BALDNESS.
I'LL HAVE YOU KNOW WOMEN FIND ME IRRESISTIBLY--

...BALD?
NOBODY LIKES BALD PEOPLE, THEY REEK OF DEATH.
HERE, JUST TAKE MY RUG...
PLOP

LUCKILY I ALWAYS CARRY A SPARE.
AND IN CASE YOUR CARPET MATCHES THE DRAPES, I'VE GOT A SPARE MERKIN, TOO.
SMUCK
...
YES, WELL, LET ME INTRODUCE YOU TO THE REST OF MY CREW...

THIS IS LIEUTENANT WOR--
KLINGON!
!
SHREE

THAT WAS MY SECURITY OFFICER...!
THEN YOUR SECURITY HAS BEEN INFILTRATED...BY KLINGONS!
AT LEAST I THINK HE'S KLINGON. THAT FOREHEAD IS ALL CRAZY AND--

DADDY! DADDY!
GAH!
SHREE

SORRY, I...THOUGHT HE WAS A COWBOY.
THAT ONE I'M NOT SO MAD ABOUT.

THIS IS OUR COURT-APPOINTED PSYCHIATRIST, DEANNA TROI.
HELL-O, NURSE...!
I CAN SENSE YOUR THOUGHTS BECAUSE I'M AN EMPATH, WHICH IS LIKE A TELEPATH BUT NOWHERE NEAR AS USEFUL.

SENSE THOUGHTS, EH?
SO WHAT AM I THINKING...?
THAT...THAT'S DISGUSTING!
AND IMPOSSIBLE!
NOT IF YOU USE A SAWHORSE.
HEY!

JEALOUS BOYFRIEND...?
EVEN BETTER.
WHA...?
CLICK
POP

DUNH-DUNH-DUNH DUNH DUNH DUNH DUNH...
CLICK

...DUNH DUNH DUNH-DUNH...
WHAT THE HELL IS THIS THING SUPPOSED TO--

BOOMF!
...DUNH DUNH DUNH DUNH...

THAT WAS AWESOME, MR. KIRK!
I AM SO BLOGGING ABOUT THIS!
COULD YOU TEACH ME TO BE COOL LIKE YOU?
GET ME A SHOT AT YOUR HOT DOCTOR MOM AND YOU'RE ON.

BOTH KINDS OF SHOTS LATER...
NO ONE *HIC* NO ONE UNNER-SHTANDS ME LIKE *HIC* LIKE DESE GREEN BISHES!
HEY, WESLEY, HAS ANYONE EVER TOLD YOU YOUR BARTENDER LOOKS LIKE WHOOPI GOLDBERG?

SHORTLY...
...AND THIS IS THE HOLODECK, WHERE YOU CAN SIMULATE ANY SETTING, PERSONAL INTERACTION OR CLICHÉ.
CAN THEY BE NAKED?
WELL, YES, BUT I DO NOT SEE WHY THAT WOULD BE NECESSARY...

MEANWHILE, ON THE BRIDGE...
CAPTAIN'S LOG, STAR-DATE: 23-87-POINT--

BYOOOO...
WHAT THE DEVIL...?!?

BYOOOO...
STATUS REPORT--
ENGAGE!
MASSIVE POWER DRAIN TO THE FLUX CAPACITOR OR SOME SH-T.

HERE'S THE SOURCE, CAPTAIN.
HOLO DECK
THE HOLODECK, EH?
DATA AND SHERLOCK HOLMES MUST BE SOLVING A PARTICULARLY PERPLEXING CASE.
LET'S HAVE A PEEK...

FSSH
WHAT THE...DATA?!?
011000100110111101101111011
0001001100110110001001
101111011011110110001001110
01101100010011011101101111
01100010011100110110001
00110111101101111011
HE MUST HAVE SEEN SOMETHING THAT FRIED HIS POSITRONIC CIRCUITS...BUT WHAT?

DAMMIT, KIRK...!
HEY, DID YOU KNOW HELEN KELLER WAS A LEFTY?
CENSORED
ALERT: ALL OFFICERS PUT ON PANTS AND REPORT TO THE BRIDGE.

ONE EXPOSITORY VIEWSCREEN CONVERSATION LATER...
WE'VE JUST RECEIVED URGENT NEWS FROM STARFLEET... THE FEDERATION IS UNDER ATTACK.
IT'S THAT NO-GOOD SPACE LINCOLN AGAIN, ISN'T IT?
WE CROSSED SWORDS SO OFTEN THAT EVENTUALLY I HAD TO GO BACK IN TIME AND ASSASSINATE HIM...

650 YEARS EARLIER...
SIC SEMPER TIBERIUS!
URK!
SHREE

DIDN'T WORK, AND WHEN I GOT BACK ALL THE MONEY HAD CHANGED.
WEIRD, RIGHT?
IT STAYED THIS WAY EVEN WHEN WE WENT BACK IN TIME AGAIN AND KILLED CHARLIE CHAPLIN.

JOINING US IN THIS BRIEFING WILL BE BENJAMIN SISKO, THE CAPTAIN OF...WELL, A SPACE TRUCKSTOP, REALLY.
MY BRUTHA'!
WORD.
POUND

AND THIS IS KATHRYN JANEWAY, THE CAPTAIN OF--
PBBBBT!

...IS THERE A PROBLEM WITH A WOMAN BEING A CAPTAIN, CAPTAIN?
COUGH
NO, NO PROBLEM, PRINCESS...NOW HOW ABOUT YOU GO 'CAPTAIN' ME UP A FRESH DRINK?
TINK TINK

THERE'LL BE TIME FOR JANEWAY TO SERVE US DRINKS LATER--WE MUST ATTEND TO THE PRESENT THREAT: THE BORG.
THEIR MOTHER SHIP IS THIS DEATH STAR TYPE VESSEL, BUT SQUARE SO THAT LUCAS' LAWYERS CAN ALL GO SUCK IT.
TO DEFEAT THE BORG WE MUST DESTROY IT... BUT HOW?

LET'S JUST GO BACK IN TIME AND GET SOME WHALES TO FIGHT IT.
THAT DID THE TRICK LAST TIME A BIG BLACK SPACE-SHIP ATTACKED EARTH.
ABSOLUTELY NOT...THANKS TO YOU AND THAT FOURTH MOVIE, STARFLEET HAS MORE THAN ENOUGH WHALES.

OOO-EEEEEE-
URRRRRRRRR
RR-OH
CLICK
I'LL TAKE IT IN MY OFFICE.

THEN WE HAVE NO CHOICE...I'LL HAVE TO CONFRONT THE BORG *MYSELF*.
THAT'S *NOT* HOW WE DO THINGS ANYMORE...FIRST WE SIT DOWN AND *TALK,* THEN TALK SOME MORE, THEN I HAVE SOME TEA AND LOOK AT MY FISH, THEN--
ONE TO BEAM OVER!
AAAND... BEAM-O!

VNNN
DAMMIT!
RAISE THE SHIELDS SO HE CAN'T COME BACK.

HALT!
PREPARE TO BE PRODDED AND ASSIMILATED.
THERE'S *NOTHING* YOU CAN DO TO THIS BODY THAT I HAVEN'T PAID YOUNG THAI GIRLS TO DO.
FREEDOM IS IRRELEV--WAIT, *WHAT* DID HE JUST SAY?

WE WILL NOW TAKE YOU TO OUR *QUEEN*.
SULU'S HERE TOO?
YOU WILL BE ASSIMILATED INTO THE COLLECTIVE...

"...JUST LIKE THE KLINGONS..."
"...THE FERENGI..."
"...AND THE TRIBBLES."
COO!
COO!*
*"RESISTANCE IS FUTILE."

OOO...HEY, WHO'S THE LOOKER?
SMALL WORDS FROM A SMALL BEING.
NOT WHERE IT COUNTS, SUGAR BYTES.
...WHAT?

YOU KNOW, YOU'RE VERY BEAUTIFUL.
R-REALLY...?
NO ONE'S EVER BEEN ABLE TO SEE PAST MY HEAD-TUBES BEFORE.
SWEETHEART, I'VE GOT USES FOR HEAD TUBES YOU'VE NEVER DREAMED OF.

LET'S JUST SLIP YOU INTO SOMETHING MORE COMFORTABLE AND WE'LL--
ZZZIP!
WUH-OH.
PLOP

KIRK, THIS IS PICARD, YOU DID IT! THE BORG SHIP IS POWERING DOWN!
SLUMP
BUT...BUT THERE'S STILL GOING TO BE PRODDING, RIGHT?

...AND THAT'S HOW MY PAL JIM KIRK SAVED THE UNIVERSE.
AGAIN.
BUT WHATEVER HAPPENED TO HIM?

WOOF, YOU READY TO GO AGAIN?
...
...I'LL GIVE YOU A FEW MINUTES.
END

THE ENTERPRISE D CREW

History: In the future, all of Earth is at peace, so humans have to travel across the galaxy to find aliens they can force their will upon. After several attempts to create the greatest starship ever (all of which were defeated by low ratings), the *Enterprise D* was built and promptly staffed by some of the most boring people in the universe.

Appearances: The crew of the *Enterprise D* has always been less involved with "TTT" than their predecessors from the *Enterprise A*—however, that is primarily because they are incredibly dull. Their only appearance in the first nine years of the strip was when they mistakenly beamed Professor X up to the *Enterprise*, believing him to be Capt. Picard ("House Party," *ToyFare* #21). It seems Commander Riker had gone insane and eaten Wesley. That was all the excitement they got until Captain Kirk himself beamed onto the ship (*ToyFare* #112). Kirk did his best to stir things up onboard the *D*—giving Picard a hairpiece, killing Worf and hitting Riker with a pillow on a stick—but in the end, only the somehow-*un*eaten Wesley decided to embrace Kirk's passion for life, drink and green-skinned hookers.

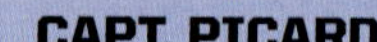
TOYFARE #21 "House Party"

CAPT. PICARD
When a battle's brewing, Jean-Luc does some brewing of his own. Brewing tea, that is! He is often mistaken for Prof. X.

COMMANDER RIKER
Beard or no beard, Will Riker is the manliest man on the *Enterprise D*, which isn't saying much. His nearest competition is bald.

LT. WORF
Recently, it was revealed that Lt. Worf was actually a Klingon and not just horribly deformed. He was promptly shot and killed.

COUNSELOR TROI
An empath from the planet Betazed, Deanna can sense your thoughts, so you should probably stop thinking what you're thinking.

DATA
This highly advanced robot has a chip he can put in his head that allows him to display emotion; he also plays cassettes.

WESLEY CRUSHER
Basically the *Enterprise*'s intern, Wesley was for some reason allowed to pilot a multi-billion dollar starship. He is also delicious.

Up and Adamantium

As originally published in *ToyFare* #106

"Every once in a while something so outlandish comes out of a 'TTT' meeting that I can't even remember how the idea originated. I'm pretty sure the infamous Alan Moore/Oscar Wilde fight spun out of someone mentioning that Wilde quote, but everything after that is a blur. At no point did anyone say, 'Wait, that's totally bizarre and has nothing to do with the plot.' But in a perfect world, the fight would have gone on for another page or two."

- Justin Aclin, "Twisted ToyFare" Writer

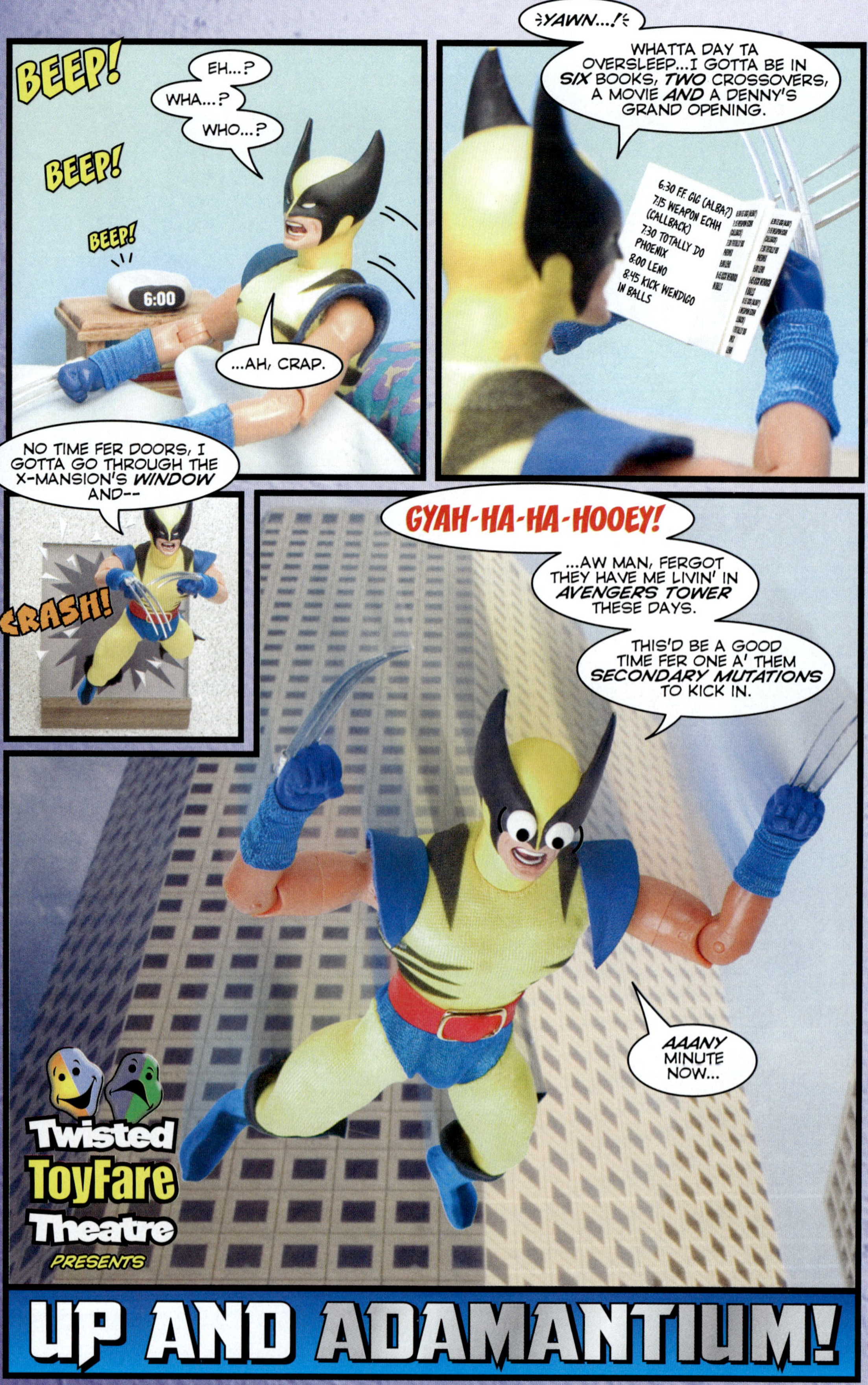

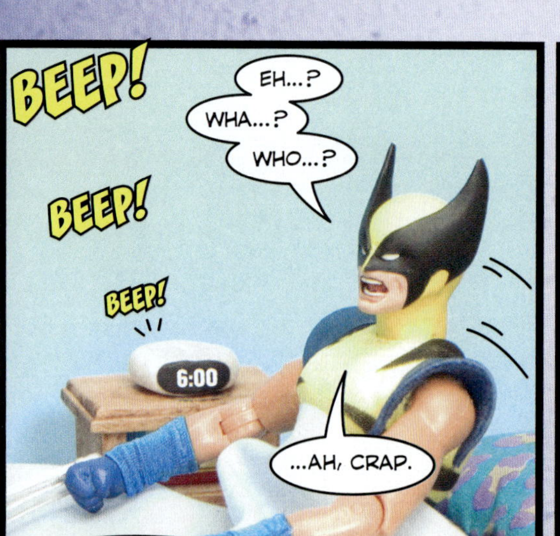

NO TIME FER DOORS, I GOTTA GO THROUGH THE X-MANSION'S *WINDOW* AND--

CRASH!

GYAH-HA-HA-HOOEY!

...AW MAN, FERGOT THEY HAVE ME LIVIN' IN *AVENGERS TOWER* THESE DAYS.

THIS'D BE A GOOD TIME FER ONE A' THEM *SECONDARY MUTATIONS* TO KICK IN.

AAANY MINUTE NOW...

Twisted ToyFare Theatre PRESENTS

UP AND ADAMANTIUM!

AHHH...!
WHY DOESH THE EIGHTH BEER OF THE MORNING ALWAYSH TASTE BETTER THAN THE FIRST?

WHOOSH!
THANKS, BUB!

HEY, SHUPERMAN... COME BACK WITH MY BEER!

¡JESÚS ME SALVE!
MAGA ZINES
WHAM!

...OW.
MOMMY, I WANT THAT MAGAZINE...THE ONE WITH WOLVERINE ON THE COVER!
WIZARD

WE GET IT-- YOU HAVE A HEALING FACTOR.
YOU'RE NOT IMPRESSING ANYONE.
I AINT GOT TIME FER YER LIP... I'M ALREADY LATE FOR MY TEAM-UP WITH THE 'ALL NEW, ALL DIFFERENT FANTASTIC FOUR.'

HEY, THEY STUCK ME ON THAT TEAM, TOO.
WANNA SPLIT A CAB?
'KAY, BUT YOU SHOULD FLAG IT DOWN...THEY DON'T STOP FOR ME ANYMORE.

THE BAXTER BUILDING, 6:23 AM...
SO SOMEONE TELL ME HOW THIS MAKES SENSE AGAIN?
WE HAVE BEEN DRAWN TOGETHER TO FIND THE ORIGINAL FANTASTIC FOUR AND--
RHARGHH!
EVERY GIRL CRAZY ABOUT SHARP DRESSED HULK!
YAY!
ARE YOU MY NEW DADDY?
MAYBE.
I DID DO YOUR MOM.
WELL, THIS HAS BEEN A THIN SLICE OF HEAVEN, BUT ACCORDING TO MY SCRIPT I HAVE TO GO STAB A VAMPIRE WITH MY CLAWS AND EAT HIS FACE.
UH, I THINK MAYBE WE SWITCHED SCRIPTS.
...GOD, I HOPE SO.
'SPIDER-MAN: THE OTHER'
WEAPON X
SHORTLY...
MORE WHEATCAKES, DEAR?
...I GUESS THIS WAS SPIDEY'S SCRIPT.
UH-OH, THAT MEANS HE'S IN ONE A' MY STORIES...
NOW TO INJECT YOU WITH MY WARM, GOOEY FORMULA, MAKE YOUR BONES ROCK HARD AND THEN STRIP YOU NAKED AND LET YOU LOOSE IN THE WOODS!
...IS JUDD WINICK WRITING THIS?
THE X-MANSION, 8:30 AM...
TO ME, MY X-MEN!
...WE'RE RIGHT HERE.
SHUT UP, SCOTT, I HAVE IMPORTANT NEWS!

I CAN WALK!
GASP!
HOW DID IT HAPPEN, PROFESSOR?
LET'S SAY NANITES THIS TIME.

A'IGHT, I GOT MY SCRIPT BACK AND I'M BEHIND SCHEDULE.
LET'S MAKE THIS QUICK.
KICK!
KRACK!

SMOOCH!

I DON'T PLAY BY YOUR RULES, BUB!

GRRR...!
I CAN BARELY CONTAIN MY BERSERKER RAGE!

SMOOCH!

FASTBALL SPECIAL, PETE!
CRASH!
DA, TOVARISH!

TO CANADA, BUB, AND STEP ON IT.

VRMM

VRMM

VRMM
...I DO NOT THINK HE IS COMING BACK.

THE U.S./CANADIAN BORDER, 10:30 AM...
YOU HAVE ANYTHING TO DECLARE?
DO I...!
I'M THE BEST THERE IS AT WHAT I DO, BUT WHAT I DO ISN'T VERY NICE. I DON'T MAKE APOLOGIES FOR WHAT I'VE DONE, FOR WHAT I AM...WHAT THEY MADE ME. IF THEY DIDN'T WANT TO GET CUT, MAYBE THEY SHOULDN'T HAVE GIVEN ME CLAWS....

2:36 PM
...MAN OR BEAST? IT'S ALL THE SAME, HUNTER, PREY... WE ALL HAVE A ROLE TO FILL. I'M JUST THE GUY THEY SEND WHEN IT GOES BAD, AND ALL I KNOW IS BAD. SO IF YOU SEE ME COMIN', IT'S ALREADY TOO LATE. I'M HELL ON WHEELS, BABY, NO APOLOGIES, NO MERCY.
ZZZZZ...
ALSO, I HAVE SOME BANANAS IN THE TRUNK, AND THAT'S IT.

DEPARTMENT PREPARATION H, 3:03 PM...
THAT'S A GREAT COSTUME, NORTHSTAR!
CHOOSING TWO COLORS WITH SUCH A STRONG CONTRAST WAS A GOOD CHOICE!
SLAM!
WOW, THANKS, I FEEL VINDICATED!
NOT SO FAST...!

HEY, WOLVERINE!
ARE YOU HERE TO JOIN ALPHA FLIGHT?
YOU WISH, VINDICATOR.
I'M HERE FOR THE... LET'S SEE, THE FRENCH-CANADIAN WHO GETS SPECIAL POWERS WHEN HE HOLDS HANDS WITH HIS SISTER AND WHO USED TO BE A MYTHICAL FAIRY BUT NOW IS JUST GAY.
ENEMY OF THE STATE
HEY, THAT'S ME!

MARK MILLAR SAYS 'BONJOUR.'
HURK...!
STAB!

NOW WHICH ONE OF YOU'S THE MIDGET?

3:45 PM
MUNCH
MUNCH

3:47 PM
NINJAS!

3:55 PM
FOOLISH WOLVERINE...YOU COULD NEVER DEFEAT MAGNETO, THE MASTER OF MAGNETISM!
I CAN CONTROL THE ADAMANTIUM WHICH LACES YOUR ENTIRE SKELETON... I CAN EVEN MAKE YOU GIVE YOURSELF THE BIRD!

AND LIKE A HELPLESS PUPPET, ALL YOU CAN DO IS WATCH AS I PULL THAT WONDEROUS METAL FROM YOUR BONES!
URK
OOOO, THEY LOOK LIKE LITTLE METAL SPERMIES...!

THANKS, BUB.
...CRAP.
UMMM...MAYBE I DIDN'T THINK THROUGH THAT WHOLE 'TAKE THE METAL OUT/CAN'T CONTROL YOU' BUSINESS.
SNIKT!
SNIKT!

CRAP!
CRAP!
CRAP!
SNIKT!
SNIKT!
SNIKT!
BE HONEST: DOES MY UNITARD MAKE ME LOOK *FAT?*
NO, YOUR *FAT* MAKES YOU LOOK FAT.

4:58 PM...
WELCOME TO *VIRGIN AIRLINES*, GUV'NER...CAN I GET YOU ANYTHING?
TWO VIRGINS.
PLAYBILL

LONDON, 12:48 AM...
I'M HERE TA' JOIN YER *TEAM!*
FROM NOW ON WE'LL BE *WOLVERINE* AND THE...UH...*WHO* ARE YOU GUYS AGAIN?

WE'RE *NEW EXCALIBUR*, THE CHRIS CLAREMONT *FANFIC* THAT MARVEL PUBLISHES.
YABBA DABBA DOO!

...NIGHTCRAWLER?
LOOKS LIKE YOU FINALLY GOT THAT *OPERATION*, HUH?
NO, I'M *NOCTURNE*... NIGHTCRAWLER AND THE SCARLET WITCH'S DAUGHTER FROM AN *ALTERNATE REALITY*.
...UH-HUH.
MAN, I'M SO *SICK* OF FEMALE KNOCKOFFS OF ESTABLISHED CHARACTERS WHO--

AT THAT VERY MOMENT, IN A PUB IN LONDON, ENGLAND...

I'M ALAN MOORE, AND YOU SHOULD BE CAREFUL WHAT YOU WISH FOR, WOLVERINE.

AS THE GREAT WRITER OSCAR WILDE ONCE SAID, 'THE ONLY THING WORSE THAN BEING TALKED ABOUT IS NOT BEING TALKED ABOU--'

I NEVER SAID THAT...!

YOUR MAGICKS ARE NO MATCH FOR *ME*, *SPELLCASTER!*
I'M A-GO *WILDE* ON YOU!
UN...*LIKELY!*

GAH...!
HIKEEBA!
ZZZZT!

AND *THAT'S* WHAT'LL HAPPEN TO THE *NEXT* MOTHER&%$#ER WHO ASKS ME ABOUT '*WATCHMEN 2*'!

OSAKA, JAPAN, 4:26 AM...
HAPPY *BIRTHDAY*, WOLVERINE... READY TO *DIE?!?*
I'M NOT AFRAID OF YOU, *POP-POP!*

...WAIT, 'POP-POP'?
I THOUGHT *YOU* WERE *MY* DAD.
WE'RE DEFINITELY *NOT* BROTHERS THOUGH, RIGHT?
MAN, EVEN *I* CAN'T KEEP UP WITH THIS CRAP...

SHORTLY...
...OKAY, I DON'T THINK WE'RE RELATED, BUT APPARENTLY I'M AN EFFEMINATE TURN-OF-THE-CENTURY TEENAGER.
HA, NICE *NIGHTSHIRT*, MARGARET!

AVENGERS TOWER, 5:59 AM...
MAN, WHAT A DAY.
I'M THE BEST THERE IS AT GOING THE HELL TO *SLEEP*.
5:59

5:59
ZZZZZZ

BEEP!
BEEP!
BEEP!
6:00
SOCCER MOM--!
...OH, FER--!

LET'S SEE WHAT I GOTTA-- *THREE* COSMIC CROSSOVERS?
MAN, I DON'T EVEN KNOW WHERE THE BADOON *LIVE!*
6:10 SECRET WAR
6:45 CIVIL WAR
7:30 INFINITY WAR
9:00 INFINITY CRUSADE
10:20 INDIANA JONES AND THE LAST CRUSADE
12:10 NACHOS BELL GRANDE
WHAT I WOULDN'T DO TO BE A LITTLE *LESS* FREAKIN' POPULAR...

AT THAT MOMENT, ACROSS TOWN IN THE NEW WARRIORS LOFT HEADQUARTERS...
MAYBE...MAYBE *TODAY'S* THE DAY 'MARVEL TEAM-UP' WILL CALL...

WHAT'D I TELL YOU?
OSCAR EFFIN' WILDE!
END

ALAN MOORE

Height: 8 inches
Weight: 1.9 oz.
Favorite Eats: Stove Top Potatoes and Stuffing, Spider-Ham
First Appearance: "Mego Super Heroes: Secret War," *ToyFare* #60
Died: "Mego Super Heroes: Secret War," *ToyFare* #60
Died: "I Am Legend, Part One," *ToyFare* #84
History: Yeah, yeah...he's the genius behind *Watchmen*, *Miracleman* and *League of Extraordinary Gentlemen*. But can he snap a man's knees when it's all on the line? That's what the "Twisted ToyFare" writing staff wanted to know when they introduced the meanest, hairiest sumbitch around, Mego Alan Moore. His superpowers at first seemed limited to showing up whenever someone confuses Man-Thing with Swamp Thing (*ToyFare* #60), but in later appearances he displayed magical abilities far beyond those of any of his contemporaries. Yes, even Grant Morrison. When he's not worshipping a Roman snake god named Glycon (read about it on Wikipedia!), Mego Alan Moore often throws down with witty Victorian playwrights—to the death! In "Up And Adamantium" (*ToyFare* #106), Moore has a karate rumble with Oscar Wilde after...actually, you just had to be there.

Needless to say, Moore went "Kid Miracleman" on his ass, inspiring his next trippy, obtuse spoken word album: "The Post-Modern Pebble in the Square Round Room of Snake Mountain." Yeah, we don't get it either.
Fighting Style: Moore is equally adept at smashing a pint glass over an opponent's head or smiting them with his mighty Magicks. He also keeps a knife in his beard, just in case.

TOYFARE #60 "Mego Superheroes: The Secret Wars"

TOYFARE #84 "I Am Legend, Part 1"

SUPER VILLAIN JEOPARDY

As originally published in *ToyFare* #1

"'The Spider Macarena' [in the *ToyFare* Spring Special] was a huge hit. So [then Editor-in-Chief] Pat McCallum said that we've gotta figure out a way to do this more often. Even though it was a little bit of a strain on the budget, 'Super Villian Jeopardy' was probably the highest-quality set we ever built. Back then we weren't into planning a whole universe. We were just like, 'Hey, let's have a good time!' Spider-Man kind of became the star of the sketch over time because his apathetic attitude allowed us to comment on things through him. It wasn't really planned."

- Doug Goldstein

BY:
McCALLUM, ROOT & GOLDSTEIN

WITH:
OAT & ACLIN

...O-KAY.
M.O.D.O.K., YOU'RE STILL IN THE LEAD, SO YOU'LL START OFF THIS ROUND OF DOUBLE JEOPARDY.
HERE ARE THE CATEGORIES...

WWII SLEEPERS
MARVEL COMICS ACRONYMS
COSMIC CUBE MISHAPS
$200
$200
$200

TINY-LIMBED VILLAINS
FAMOUS EX-BELLHOPS
PLUS-SIZE HATS
$200
$200
$200

OOOH... I'LL TAKE MARVEL ACRONYMS FOR $400.

"THIS TERRORIST ORGANIZATION WEARS YELLOW BEE-KEEPER OUTFITS AND CREATED M.O.D.O.K."
WHAT IS A.I.M.?
BUZZ!
BUZZ!
CLICK
$600
$1400
$2.49
M.O.D.O.K.
DOOM

"THIS SUPREME HEADQUARTERS IS RUN BY COLONEL NICK FURY."
UN VHAT IS S.H.I.E.L.D.?
BUZZ!
BUZZ!
CLICK CLICK
$600
$1800
$2.49
RED

"THIS SO-CALLED 'CAPTAIN MARVEL' IS IN FACT NOT A MARVEL CHARACTER AT ALL!"
WHO IS SHAZAM?
BUZZ!
BUZZ!
CLICK
CLICK
CLICK
$1800
$2.49

SOMEONE HAS TAMPERED WITH DOOM'S WIRES!

WHO DARES TO--EH, WHAT'S THIS...?

A KNIFE?!?
INSOLENT FREAK, YOU DARE MEDDLE IN THE AFFAIRS OF DOOM?!?
OH, FOR...

IT'S A WWII-ISSUE KNIFE, IT'S GOT A SKULL ON IT, AND EVEN IF I WANTED TO USE IT, MY ARMS ARE TOO SHORT!
BLAME THE GERMAN.

AND ANOTHER THING...WOULD YOU PLEASE STOP TALKING IN THE THIRD PERSON?
IT'S SOOOO ANNOY--HEY, WHATTYA DOIN'?
HEY!

UH... HMMM.
I'M, UH... I'M A LITTLE STUCK. SOMEONE WANNA GIVE ME A HAND?
WOBBLE
WOBBLE

CONSIDER MR. POTATO HEAD'S WINNINGS THE PROPERTY OF DOOM.
YOU MAY NOW CONTINUE.
...I'M GETTING A NOSE BLEED.
$2600
$2.

OKAY, LET'S TRY AND GET THIS OVER WITH AND MOVE ON TO FINAL JEOPARDY.
CONTESTANTS, HERE'S YOUR QUESTION...

"THIS MARVEL COMICS VILLAIN IS RUMORED TO BE A DESCENDANT OF RAMA-TUT."
BUZZ!
BUZZ!
$2600

"DR. DOOM, YOU BUZZED IN FIRST."
THE ANSWER...IS DOOM.

OOOH, NO, I'M SORRY.
THE ANSWER IS 'WHO IS DOOM?'
BUT WE HAVE SOME *LOVELY* PARTING GIF--

DOOM SHALL NOT BE PLACATED WITH THE HOME GAME!

WHOA, HEY, TAKE...TAKE IT EASY...
AIEEE!
AND DOOM NEED *NOT* PHRASE HIS ANSWERS IN THE FORM OF *QUESTIONS!*
$1200
RED SKULL
$2600
M.O.D.O.K.

"SECURITY! *SECURITY!!!*"
C'MON, PONCH!
I'LL PUT HIM IN AN *'ESTRADA'* JACKET...GET IT?

STAY DOWN, PERP!
CLANG!
UH...HEY, JON, WE ON CAMERA?
THIS IS ALL RICHARDS' FAULT!
RICHARDS!!!
END

"TONIGHT'S 'JEOPARDY' WAS BROUGHT TO YOU BY..."

M.O.D.O.C.K.E.R.S.

Mental Organism Designed Only for Chinos and Khakis with Extra Room in the Seat

PARDODY

ALEX TREBEK

Height: What is "7.5 inches tall?"
Weight: What is "2.3 ounces?"
Occupation: Megoville TV Host, Elite Class
Headquarters: Soundstage 34, Studio City, Megoville
First Appearance: "Super Villain Jeopardy," *ToyFare* #1
Died: "Viva Mego!" *ToyFare* #33
Died: "I Am Legend, Part One," *ToyFare* #84
History: Who is "possibly the most important Megoville resident in existence?"

Locking his cold, steely eyes with readers in the first panel of the first official "Twisted ToyFare Theatre" strip ever ("Super Villain Jeopardy," *ToyFare* #1), Trebek has delighted audiences with his wry, "smarter-than-you-jerks" speaking style on shows such as Ultimate Idol (*ToyFare* #67) and Megoville's Funniest Home Videos (*ToyFare* #20). Then, suddenly, a re-launched and retconned "TTT" universe (*ToyFare* #85) rebooted existence back to *ToyFare* #1's "Supervillain Jeopardy," and Trebek realized how tenuous his control over his own destiny was. Trebek vowed his existence would not be threatened again in such a way. Rival Megoville host Ryan Seacrest was suddenly murdered under bizarre circumstances. Soon, Megoville's Pat Sajak, Burt Convey and Peter Tomarken would fall to Trebek's life-wrenching hands. Though tiny blue answer cards (under the category "There Can Be Only One" for $200) were found at the crime scene, Trebek was never charged with the killings. Ironically, he escaped prison time under Megoville's "Double Jeopardy" laws.

Weapons: A dry wit, a wink and a smile. Also, a razor sharp boot knife in the heel of his Italian wing tips.

TOYFARE #67 "Idol Hands"

TOYFARE #85 "I Am Legend, Part 2"

THE WAY WE WUZ

As originally published in *ToyFare* #64

"This was the first strip that our current 'TTT' designer Eric Goodman worked on, and I just remember seeing the panel where the Fantastic Four are using their powers and everyone going, 'Wow...that actually looks really good!' Over time we've probably come to rely too much on Eric, sometimes creating strips where every panel needs Photoshop, but it's Eric's own fault for setting the bar so high his first time out."

- Justin Aclin

Twisted ToyFare Theatre

PRESENTS

THE WAY WE WUZ

HEAD WRITERS: McCALLUM, ROOT & OAT

CONTRIBUTING WRITERS: BRICKEN, PATYK, GUTIERREZ & ACLIN

STORY EDITORS: GOLDSTEIN & SENREICH

CAPTAIN AMERICAR SUPPLIED BY: ANDREW KARDON

ANTE UP, YA MARYS!

BENJY NEEDS A NEW PAIR'A HOOKERS!

GAMBLING IS *IMMORAL*, SO I'M BETTING WITH JELLY BEANS.

I HOPE NO ONE MINDS.

IT'S A GOOD THING I TURNED OFF MY *OLFACTORY SENSORS* THE SECOND THE *HULK* REACHED FOR THAT BEAN DIP.

I'M BEING *BOMBARDED.*

"REED INSISTED WE BRING ALONG HIS GAL AND HER KID BRUDDA. HE SAID IN CASE WE WUZ MAROONED WE'D NEED SOMEONE TA POPULATE DA MOON AND SOMEONE TA EAT."
THERE'S A HOLE IN MY SUIT...I THINK SPACE IS GETTING IN!
WE THERE YET?
THIS IS SO GONNA RULE!

"SUDDENLY, TH' SHIP WUZ BOMBARDED BY DAT CRAZY COSMIC RADIATION!"
ASSUME THE CRASH POSITION... EVERYONE PUT YOUR HEAD BETWEEN YOUR LEGS!
TEE-HEE!
BEN, I SAID YOUR LEGS!

"TH' COSMIC RAYS GAVE US FANTASTICAL POWERS! REED DECIDED WE SHOULD FIGHT CRIME, WHICH WAS IRONIC CONSIDERIN' OUR ENORMOUS FEDERAL OFFENSE."
"REED BECAME DA AMAZING MR. FANTASTIC!"
"SUE WAS DA SPECTACULAR INVISIBLE WOMAN!"
"JOHNNY WAS DA STUPENDOUS HUMAN TORCH!"
"THEY CALLED ME THE THING."

...
I SHOULD'A KILLED 'EM ALL IN DEIR SLEEP DAT NIGHT.

WELL, MY ORIGIN ISN'T QUITE AS SENSATIONAL, BUT IT STILL--
WAIT, WAIT-- LEMME SEE IF I CAN GUESS...

"I WAS JUST A SCRAWNY TEENAGER WHEN THE GOVERNMENT INJECTED ME WITH THE *SUPER SOLDIER SERUM*..."

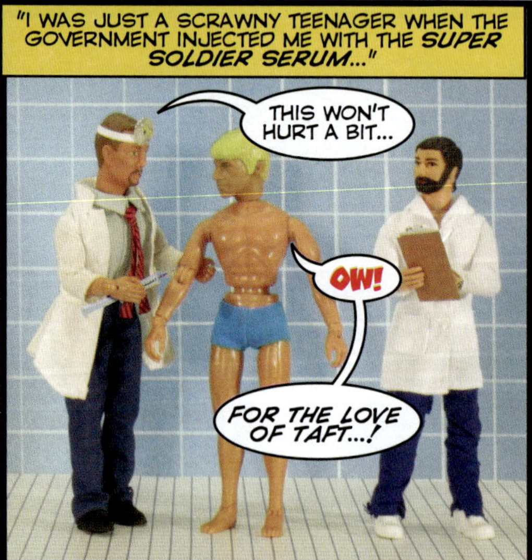

"PUMPED UP ON *ARTIFICIAL GROWTH DRUGS*, MY FIRST ORDER OF BUSINESS WAS TO TOPPLE MAJOR LEAGUE BASEBALL'S *HOME RUN RECORD*."

"THE PLAYER'S STRIKE IN EFFECT, I BECAME *CAPTAIN AMERICA!* WITH MY SIDEKICK, *BUCKY*, WE DEFEATED ALL THE WORLD'S EVILS, LIKE *HITLER*, AND WOMEN'S LIBERATION."

DAT'S *YER* ORIGIN, BUT WHERE'D DIS *BUCKY* KID COME FROM?
...UMMM...

HEY KID, WANT A RIDE? I'VE GOT CANDY...
HOT DOG!
CAPTAIN AMERICA

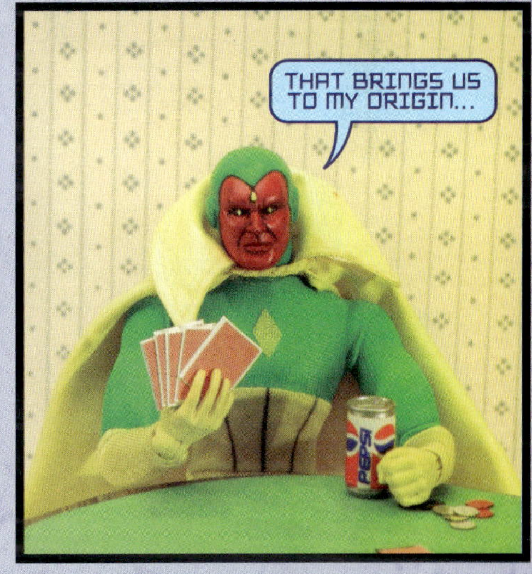
THAT BRINGS US TO MY ORIGIN...
PEPSI

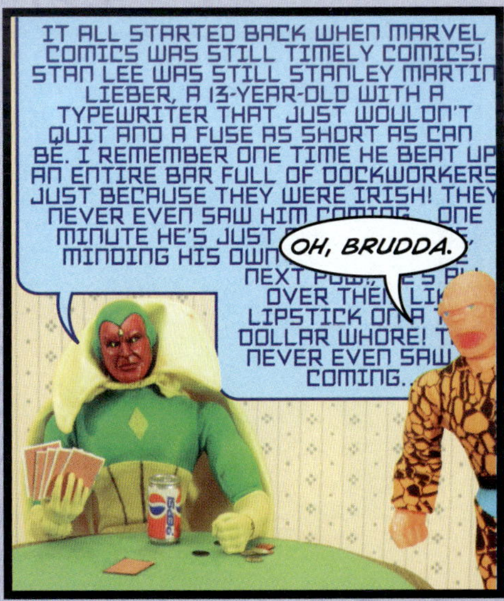
IT ALL STARTED BACK WHEN MARVEL COMICS WAS STILL TIMELY COMICS! STAN LEE WAS STILL STANLEY MARTIN LIEBER, A 13-YEAR-OLD WITH A TYPEWRITER THAT JUST WOULDN'T QUIT AND A FUSE AS SHORT AS CAN BE. I REMEMBER ONE TIME HE BEAT UP AN ENTIRE BAR FULL OF DOCKWORKERS JUST BECAUSE THEY WERE IRISH! THEY NEVER EVEN SAW HIM ... ONE MINUTE HE'S JUST ... MINDING HIS OWN ... NEXT ... OVER THE ... LIPSTICK ON A ... DOLLAR WHORE! ... NEVER EVEN SAW ... COMING...
OH, BRUDDA.

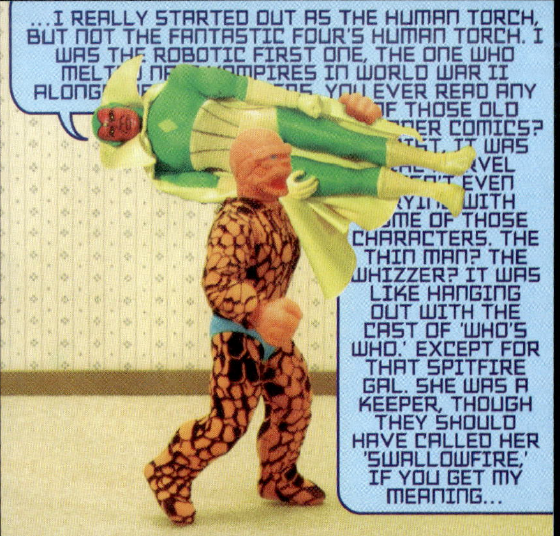
...I REALLY STARTED OUT AS THE HUMAN TORCH, BUT NOT THE FANTASTIC FOUR'S HUMAN TORCH. I WAS THE ROBOTIC FIRST ONE, THE ONE WHO MELT... VAMPIRES IN WORLD WAR II ALONG... YOU EVER READ ANY OF THOSE OLD ... COMICS? ... IT WAS ... EVEN ... WITH ... OF THOSE CHARACTERS. THE THIN MAN? THE WHIZZER? IT WAS LIKE HANGING OUT WITH THE CAST OF 'WHO'S WHO.' EXCEPT FOR THAT SPITFIRE GAL. SHE WAS A KEEPER, THOUGH THEY SHOULD HAVE CALLED HER 'SWALLOWFIRE,' IF YOU GET MY MEANING...

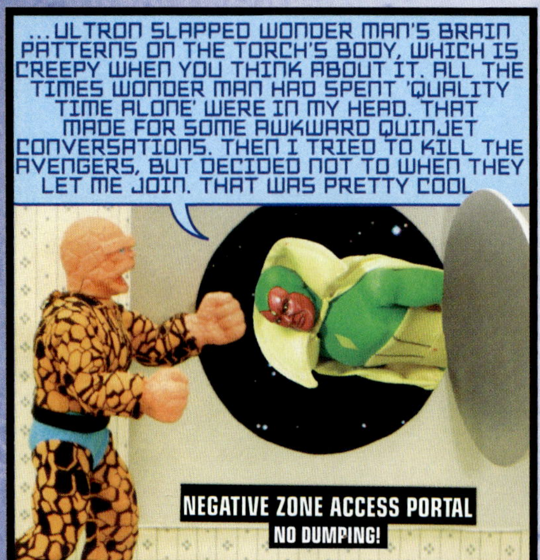
...ULTRON SLAPPED WONDER MAN'S BRAIN PATTERNS ON THE TORCH'S BODY, WHICH IS CREEPY WHEN YOU THINK ABOUT IT. ALL THE TIMES WONDER MAN HAD SPENT 'QUALITY TIME ALONE' WERE IN MY HEAD. THAT MADE FOR SOME AWKWARD QUINJET CONVERSATIONS. THEN I TRIED TO KILL THE AVENGERS, BUT DECIDED NOT TO WHEN THEY LET ME JOIN. THAT WAS PRETTY COOL...
NEGATIVE ZONE ACCESS PORTAL
NO DUMPING!

...WHEN JOHN BYRNE REVAMPED MY ORIGIN SO NOW I'M NOT THE ORIGINAL H MAN TORCH ANYMORE. MAN, I WISH HE DECIDE DO THAT BACK IN 1986 WHEN HE WAS STILL GOOD. THE WORST PART WAS I GOT STUCK WITH AN A WHITE COSTUME FOR LIKE F YEARS. I THINK I WAS BAR TOO. WHO MAKES BAREFOO SUPERHERO COSTUMES? VALIANT? YOU SEE WHERE IT GOT THEM...

NOW TIME FOR *HULK'S* ORIGIN...
MOTT'S

"IT WAS DARK AND STORMY NIGHT AT STATELY HULK MANOR..."
RHARGHH!
VILLAINS SUPERSTITIOUS AND *COWARDLY* LOT!
CRASH!
"AND THAT HOW *HULK* BECOME *BAT-HULK*."

PLEASE KEEP HULK'S IDENTITY SECRET.
MOTT'S

DAT REMINDS ME OF DA TIME--
UNCA BEN, WHAT'S *MY* ORIGIN?
CONDOMS BREAK.
ANYBODY ELSE GOTS A STORY?

WELL, I DISCOVERED *MY* POWERS IN COLLEGE.
ME AND MY ROOMMATE *TODD* HAD TOO MUCH TO DRINK ONE NIGHT AND STARTED WATCHING *'FUNNY GIRL'* --

OH, HEY, LOOKIT THE TIME...
YEAH...BIG, UH, *AVENGERS WEST COAST* MEETING TOMORROW...

SAME TIME NEXT WEEK?
SURE.
SAY...WASN'T *DAREDEVIL* SUPPOSED TO BE HERE?

AT THAT MOMENT, ACROSS TOWN...
...AND *THAT*, MY FELLOW SUPERHEROES, IN HOW *MATT MURDOCK* BECAME *DAREDEVIL, THE MAN WITHOUT FEAR.*
HEY, WHO WANTS TO KNOW *SPIDER-MAN'S* SECRET IDENTITY?
I DO!
I DO!
END

VISION

Height: 7.75 inches
Weight: 2.7 oz.
Group Affiliations: The Avengers, West Coast Avengers, Skynet
First Appearance: "Iron Resolve," *ToyFare* #7
Died: "Viva Mego!" *ToyFare* #33
Died: "'Til Death Do You Part," *ToyFare* #57
Died: "The Way We Wuz" *ToyFare* #64
Died: "I Am Legend, Part Two," *ToyFare* #85
History: Programmed not to have to follow Issac Asimov's little known fourth rule of robotics—"A robot may not hook up with a hot human woman...that's eight kinds of screwed up"—Vision thought he was headed for a sweet-ass life as a superpowered robot with an endless supply of red-headed lovin' when he married Scarlet Witch. Unfortunately, his marriage to Wanda tortures his every pathetic moment. Though the occasional make-out session (*ToyFare* #45) and swingin' three-way with Susan Richards (*ToyFare* #43) has occurred, his ice queen wife is quick to make him feel like less than a man the rest of the time. It doesn't help that he technically is less than a man. The whipped 'bot does little to stop the "emasculating she-beast" besides whining and taking his pain out on innocent robots (*ToyFare* #73). It saddens us to say his wife even gives him an allowance (*ToyFare* #63). Jesus, even *we're* starting to hate this spineless Dell Computer, whose sad dying wish is to see the Charisma Carpenter Playboy spread (*ToyFare* #84). Come on, Vision, grow a pair!
Weapons: Eye beams can easily melt the fleshy torso of Bucky (*ToyFare* #34). Drives an automatic transmission car with almost sensual precision.

TOYFARE #22 "Law is War"

TOYFARE #29 "Y2K Monkey Business"

Clash of the Titans, Part 1

As originally published in *ToyFare* #8

"There was always a huge respect for Megos, and at that time the Famous Covers toy line was released by Toy Biz as a way of reintroducing figures of that ilk. And the core fans saw a difference between them and the original Mego figures in ways that they would criticize, as core fans always do. So the idea of having the Famous Covers try to usurp the Megos' role in that category of toy was something that was going on regardless of *ToyFare*."

- Doug Goldstein

Twisted ToyFare Theatre

Clash of the Titans

By Pat McCallum, Tom Root and Douglas Goldstein

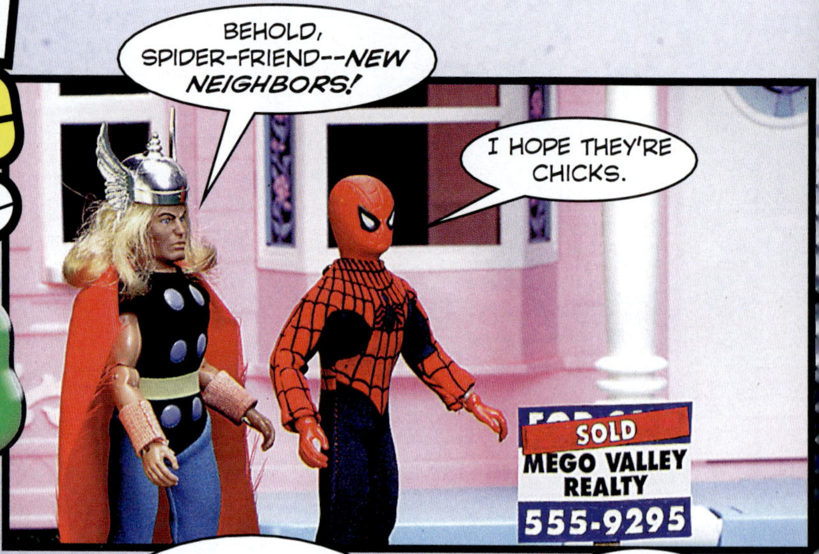

BEHOLD, SPIDER-FRIEND--*NEW NEIGHBORS!*

I HOPE THEY'RE CHICKS.

SOLD
MEGO VALLEY REALTY
555-9295

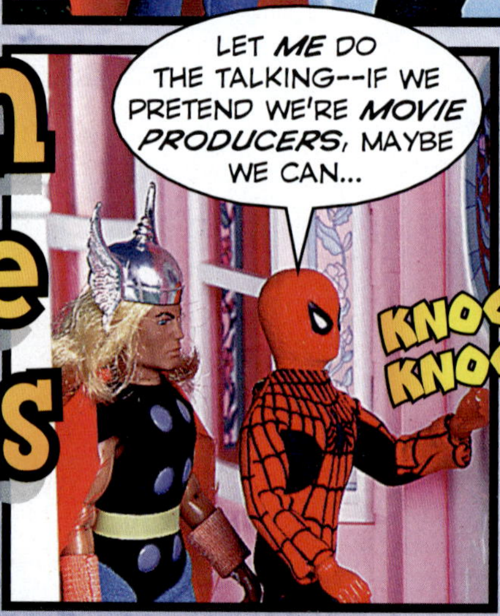

LET *ME* DO THE TALKING--IF WE PRETEND WE'RE *MOVIE PRODUCERS*, MAYBE WE CAN...

KNOCK KNOCK

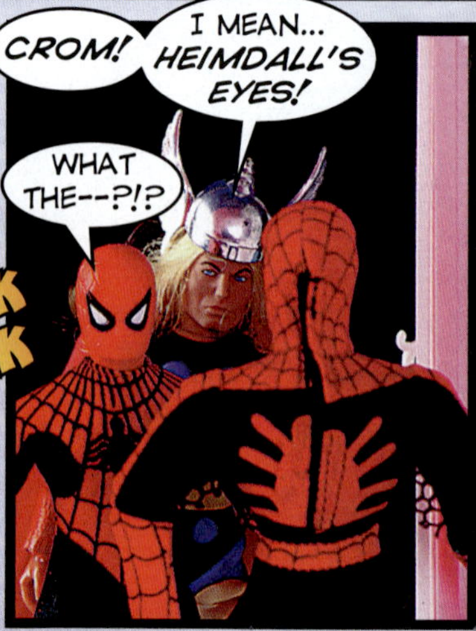

CROM!

I MEAN... *HEIMDALL'S EYES!*

WHAT THE--?!?

'FAMOUS COVERS'...?

WE'RE JUST AS POSEABLE AS YOU HAS-BEENS, WE HAVE BETTER CLOTH COSTUMES AND WE'RE NOT HELD TOGETHER WITH RUBBER BANDS.
WE'RE HELD TOGETHER WITH RUBBER BANDS?

WE CAN DO STUFF YOU ANTIQUES CAN'T EVEN DREAM OF. CAN YOU DO...*THIS?*
NOPE. CAN YOU DO...

...*THIS?*
URK--!
THOK

BIG MISTAKE, BUB!
BY THE GODDESS!
I'VE GOT A PUMPKIN.
...URRRR...

YOU GUYS WANNA THROW DOWN? FINE, BUT WE'LL SETTLE THIS THE OLD-FASHIONED WAY...

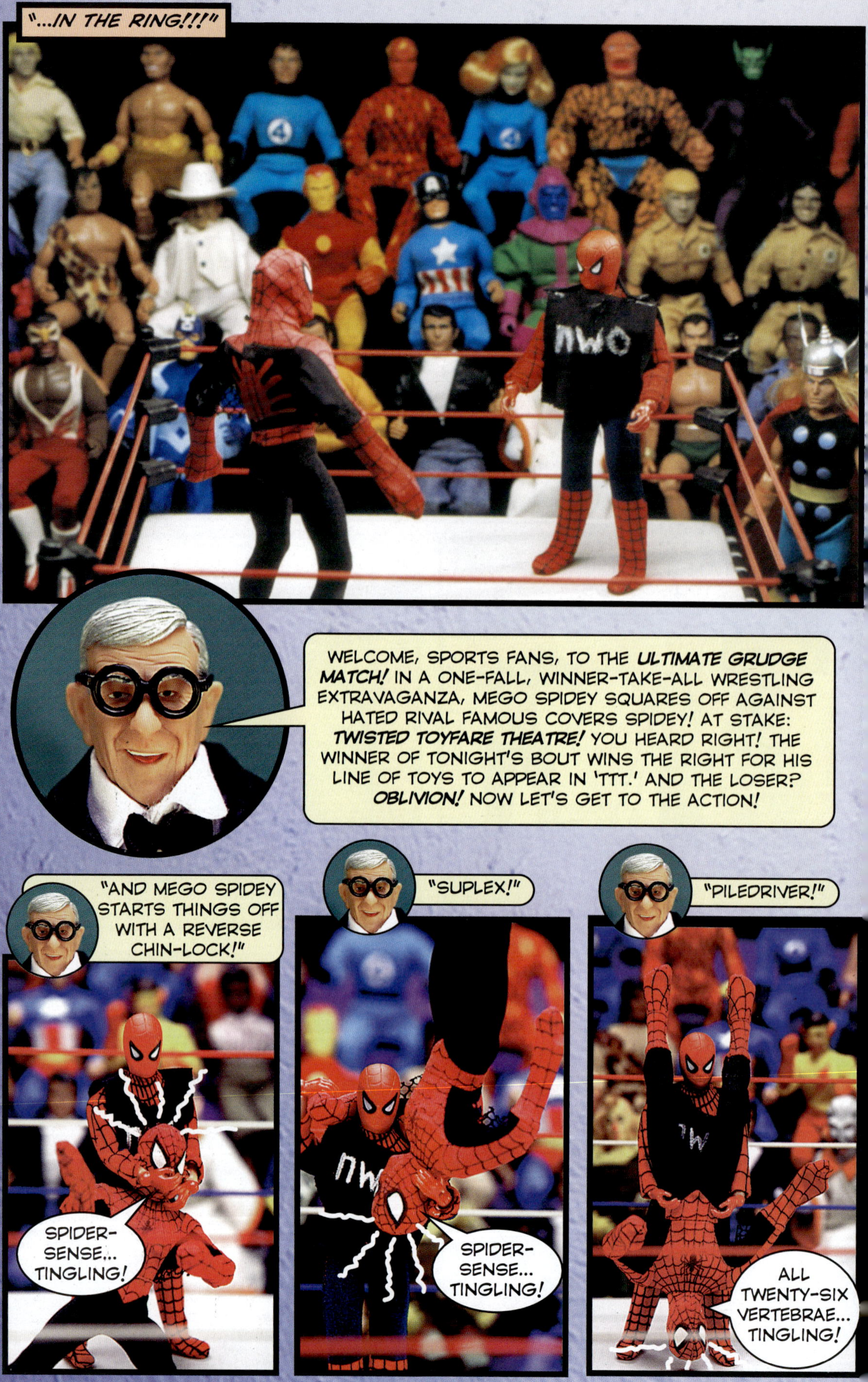

"...IN THE RING!!!"

WELCOME, SPORTS FANS, TO THE ***ULTIMATE GRUDGE MATCH!*** IN A ONE-FALL, WINNER-TAKE-ALL WRESTLING EXTRAVAGANZA, MEGO SPIDEY SQUARES OFF AGAINST HATED RIVAL FAMOUS COVERS SPIDEY! AT STAKE: ***TWISTED TOYFARE THEATRE!*** YOU HEARD RIGHT! THE WINNER OF TONIGHT'S BOUT WINS THE RIGHT FOR HIS LINE OF TOYS TO APPEAR IN 'TTT.' AND THE LOSER? ***OBLIVION!*** NOW LET'S GET TO THE ACTION!

MEANWHILE...
ALL RIGHT THEN, YOU WAGER STARK INDUSTRIES ON MEGO SPIDEY, AND I'LL PUT UP THE BOAR'S NEST ON THAT FAMOUS COVERS FELLA!
DEAL!

"WAIT...FAMOUS COVERS SPIDEY IS HULKING UP! MEGO SPIDEY COULD BE IN TROUBLE!"
HEY, THIS WASN'T IN THE SCRIPT!

MINE MEGO COMRADE ART AT A DISADVANTAGE! THE ODINSON COULD LEND ASSISTANCE... BUT DOTH HIS FRIENDSHIP EVEN HAVE VALUE? NAY, IF MEMORY DOTH SERVE THOR...
*SEE TOYFARE WINTER SPECIAL EDITION
*SEE TOYFARE SUMMER SPECIAL EDITION
*SEE TOYFARE #2

I SAY THEE NAY! THE MIGHTY THOR SHALT NEVER TURN AN UNSEEING EYE TO THE PLIGHT OF HIS EARTHLY COMPANIONS!

IF THE ODINSON IS TO ACT, HE MUST ACT NOW!
C'MON, SAY 'UNCLE'! SAY IT!
SHAZAM! UGH FLAME ON! OUCH BY THE POWER OF GREYSKULL! OW DAMN, NOTHING'S WORKING!

"WAIT...A SUDDEN REVERSAL BY MEGO SPIDEY! IT LOOKS LIKE FAMOUS COVERS SPIDEY IS GOING TO SUBMIT!"
YOUR TURN, LOSER! SAY UN
WHAK!!

"AN UNPRECEDENTED TURN OF EVENTS! FAMOUS COVERS SPIDEY COVERS MEGO SPIDEY FOR A POSSIBLE PINFALL..."
1... 2... 3!!
UHH...

FAMOUS COVERS WINS! TWISTED TOYFARE THEATRE...IS OURS!!!

NOT A HOAX! NOT A DREAM! NOT AN IMAGINARY TALE!
NEXT MONTH: FAMOUS COVERS THEATRE!
THE ODINSON ART HOPPING THE FIRST TRAIN OUT OF TOWN.
CYBERTRON AND ALL ITS MOONS BELONG TO ME!
YEE-HAW! DEFENSE CONTRACTS FOR EVERYBODY!
TO BE CONTINUED NEXT ISSUE!

Clash of the Titans, Part 2

As originally published in *ToyFare* #9

"Nothing holds less promise for humor than a statement like, 'We'll be right back with more comedy.' My second-favorite visual in this strip is how Hazzard County is as flat as a tabletop—since we shot it on a table—and how the General Lee managed to hit apparently the only tree in existence. My *favorite* visual is the blood pooling in the Famous Covers Green Goblin's eye. Incredibly disturbing."

- Tom Root

Twisted

FAMOUS COVERS MASTERPIECE THEATRE presents

Clash of the Titans Part II

By Pat McCallum, Tom Root and Douglas Goldstein

Photos by Paul Schiraldi.

SWEET MOTHER OF GOD... IT'S WORSE THAN I THOUGHT! THIS 'FAMOUS COVERS THEATRE' THING IS A TRAVESTY!

I STILL CAN'T BELIEVE WE LOST 'TWISTED TOYFARE THEATRE' TO THESE IDIOTS IN A WRESTLING MATCH.*
* SEE LAST ISH.

WHAK!!
"THINGS WERE GOING GREAT UNTIL THAT IDIOT THOR HIT ME WITH A CHAIR INSTEAD OF THAT *IMPOSTER* SPIDER-MAN."
"SO NOT ONLY DID WE LOSE 'TTT' TO THOSE FAMOUS COVERS JERKS, BUT IRON MAN BET ON THE MATCH AND LOST STARK INDUSTRIES TO BOSS HOGG. FUNNY...NO ONE'S SEEN IRON MAN OR THOR SINCE. I WONDER WHERE THEY WENT..."
AHH, WHO CARES WHERE THEY WENT? THERE'S ONLY ONE PERSON I CAN TURN TO TO HELP ME GET RID OF THESE FAMOUS COVERS DILLWEEDS...
AT THAT VERY MOMENT IN HAZZARD COUNTY...
VERILY, YON LAWMAN COLTRANE CONTINUES HIS PURSUIT.
WE'LL LOSE 'IM WHEN WE JUMP CHICKASAW CREEK! YEEEEEEE-HAW!!!

"...DR. DOOM!"
BLAST! WHENEVER DOOM IS ON THE CAN...
KNOCK KNOCK KNOCK
DAILY BUGLE
FLASH THOMPSON SCORES
DAILY BUGLE
SPIDER-MAN STILL A MENACE

IF IT BE THOSE WRETCHED TEENS AGAIN...
ALL RIGHT, ALL RIGHT, DOOM IS COMING!

MEDDLESOME ARACHNID! YOU DARE FLAUNT YOUR VISAGE AT THE HOME OF DOOM?
ENGLISH, PAL, ENGLISH.

LISTEN, THOSE FAMOUS COVERS LOSERS ARE MAKING A MOCKERY OF THINGS, AND...
..YOU DESIRE DOOM'S AID? LAUGHABLE. SHALL I TALLY THE INDIGNITIES YOU AND YOUR SLOW-WITTED ACQUAINTANCES HAVE HEADED UPON MY PERSON? YOUR PLIGHT IS NO CONCERN TO DOOM.

OH YEAH? THEN CHECK THIS OUT.
THEY DARE REPLACE DOOM?!? LO, BUT THEY SHALL PAY FOR THEIR CAPITALISTIC ARROGANCE!
DOOM
On sale soon!

AN ALLIANCE IT IS, SPIDER-MAN. YOU SHALL PROVIDE A DISTRACTION, AND DOOM...DOOM SHALL DEAL WITH THESE IMPOSTERS!

SHORTLY...
DISTRACT THEM, HUH? A BRICK THROUGH THE WINDOW OUGHTA--

HMM... CHANGE OF PLANS.
ME-MEW. ME-MEW.
KANGAROO SOUND. KANGAROO SOUND.
QUACK QUACK.
MOO. MOO.

MEANWHILE...
ALL RIGHT, WHO ATE MY PUMPKIN PIE?
MMMPH-MEH!

UH, GUYS? YOU MIGHT WANNA SEE THIS.
RIDE DOGIES, RIDE!!!
ANGRY BAA! BAA!
ANGRY MOO! MOO!
ANGRY KANGAROO SOUND! ANGRY KANGAROO SOUND!
RRRRRRRRRRRRRRRUMMMMBLE
FEED, MY BEANIE FRIENDS, FEED!
GAH!
I LIKE NUTS.
HEY... THEIR TAGS ARE STILL ON. THOSE GUYS ARE WORTH MONEY!!!

BACK AT CASTLE DOOM...
NOW, LET ALL THOSE WHO WOULD COPYRIGHT DOOM'S LIKENESS TREMBLE AS HE UNLEASHES...
...THE SPICE CANNON!!!
...'ERE NOW GOVNAH, WHOT'S 'IS?

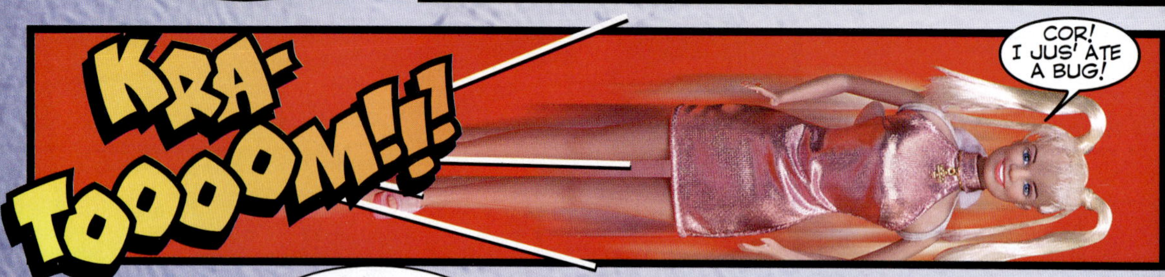
KRA-TOOOOM!!!
COR! I JUS' ATE A BUG!

I MAY BE THE LAST FAMOUS COVERS STANDING, WALL-CRAWLER, BUT I'M STILL THE BEST THERE IS AT WHAT I-- EH?
SPIDER-SENSE... TINGLIN*
WHY, GOD, WHY?

URK
SSSLARK!
OW, ME 'EAD! STUPID, UGLY AMERICAN!*
*ACTUALLY WOLVERINE IS CANADIAN. BABY SPICE IS JUST STUPID.

MAGNIFICENT! AN INSTRUMENT OF ULTIMATE DESTRUCTION AND ANNOYANCE! I --HMM?
TAP TAP

UMM...

YE'VE TANGLED WIT' OUR SISTAH, AN' NOW YE FACE...

"...GIRL POWER!!!"
THIS IS RICHARDS' FAULT! RICHARDSSSSSS...
SO ANYWAY, WHAT'VE WE LEARNED TODAY?

WELL, FOR ONE THING, BAD COMEDY IS LIKE BAD FISH --IF YOU DIGEST TOO MUCH OF IT, YOU DIE SCREAMING ON A TOILET. WE ALSO LEARNED THAT EVEN CUTE 'N' CUDDLY PETS WILL EAT JUST ABOUT ANYTHING IF YOU PEN 'EM UP LONG ENOUGH.
THAT, AND WE LEARNED BEANIE BABIES AREN'T REALLY FULL OF BEANS. WEIRD, HUH?

MEANWHILE, BACK IN HAZZARD COUNTY...
TRAGIC.
YEP. SOOO...WANNA GO SPY ON UNCLE JESSE IN THE SHOWER?
01
THE END

FAMOUS COVERS FIGURES

History: No one knows where they came from, or how they were able to afford a house in such a nice neighborhood, but the Famous Covers moved next door to Spidey's house one day...and into a starring role in "TTT" shortly afterward. They're also very tall.

Appearances: Famous Covers debuted and were defeated in the two-part story you just read—"Clash of the Titans"—and that might have been the last that anyone ever saw of them. But they resurfaced quite a long time later in *ToyFare* #84's "I Am Legend, Part 1." Here we catch up with the Famous Covers family, destitute and living in a shantytown at the edge of Megoville with their dog. Suddenly, the Famous Covers figures found themselves beaten once again, this time by Marvel Legends figures, sacrificed to the ancient storytelling art of wiping out a weak group in the beginning of the story to establish that a new enemy is tough. They haven't reappeared since.

TOYFARE #8 "Clash of the Titans"

SPIDER-MAN

Despite his removable mask, FC Spidey apparently died sometime prior to *ToyFare* #84, as he didn't appear with the rest of the team.

STORM

Famous Covers Storm is a famously fantastic cook, whether she's making cookies or shoe-and-puddle-water soup.

WOLVERINE

Much like Mego Wolverine, he's an insufferable blowhard who can't stop talking about himself. And he really likes cookies.

THE GREEN GOBLIN

He's got a pumpkin.

DR. DOOM

Not ever physically present in a strip, just the threat of the existence of FC Doom was enough to rally Mego Doom to Spidey's cause.

AUNT MAY

FC May is a grotesque monstrosity who kidnapped Mego Aunt May and took her place circa *ToyFare* #34. Seriously. Look it up!

House Party

As originally published in *ToyFare* #21

"This was our big 'It's time to make fun of the X-Men' sketch. The idea that they would be kids—having a party when Xavier is away—just felt right because we always liked to play up the fact that Xavier is like a father figure to them. He's a downer, and they're just looking to have a good time."

- Doug Goldstein

Twisted ToyFare Theatre

HOUSE PARTY

By Pat McCallum, Tom Root and Douglas Goldstein

WITHIN THE HALLOWED HALLS OF A CERTAIN WESTCHESTER MANSION THAT SERVES AS BOTH HOME AND HEADQUARTERS TO THE MUTANT BAND OF OUTLAW HEROES KNOWN AS THE *UNCANNY X-MEN*...

I HOPE YOU'RE READY TO PARTY, PAL, BECAUSE...

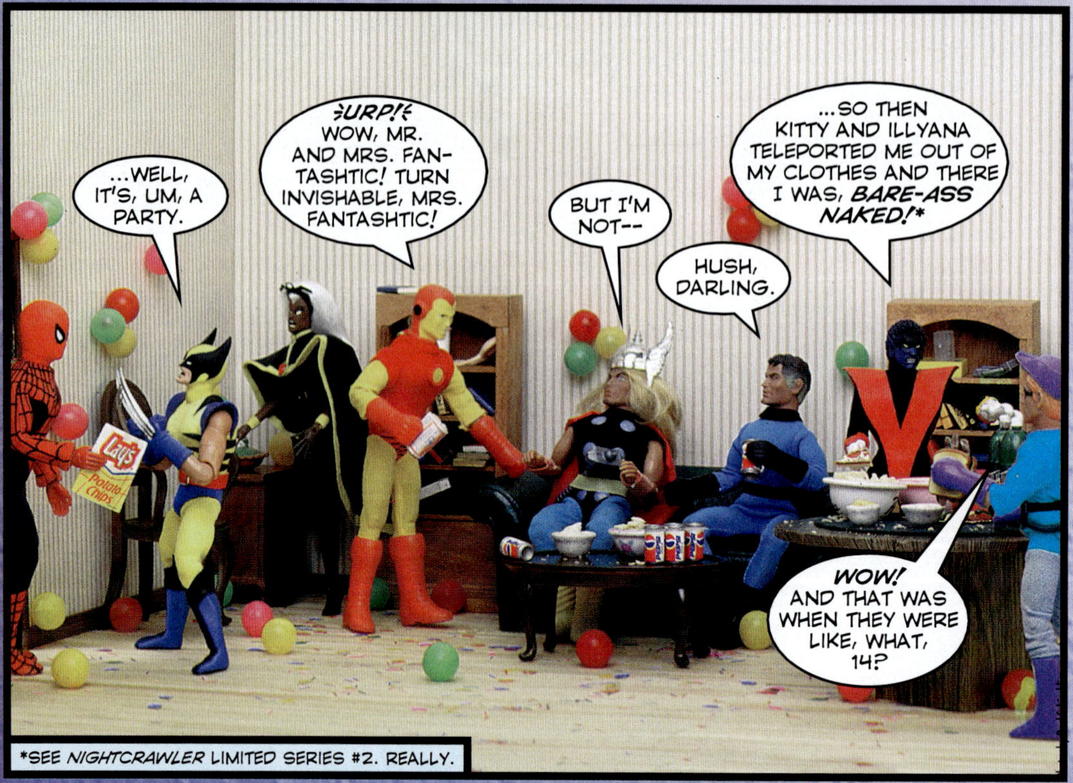

...WELL, IT'S, UM, A PARTY.

URP! WOW, MR. AND MRS. FAN-TASHTIC! TURN INVISHABLE, MRS. FANTASHTIC!

BUT I'M NOT--

HUSH, DARLING.

...SO THEN KITTY AND ILLYANA TELEPORTED ME OUT OF MY CLOTHES AND THERE I WAS, *BARE-ASS NAKED!**

WOW! AND THAT WAS WHEN THEY WERE LIKE, WHAT, 14?

*SEE *NIGHTCRAWLER* LIMITED SERIES #2. REALLY.

⋟SNIFF, SNIFF⋞ THEM RUFFLED?
I DON'T KNOW, I FOUND 'EM UNDER THE SEAT OF MY CAR.
N-NO, WAIT, MR. RASPUTIN--!
FASTBALL SPECIAL, TOVARISH! ⋟HIC⋞ DAS VADANYA!
HEY, THIS DIP'S PRETTY GOOD!
SPLAT!
MUNCH! MUNCH!

YEAH, YOU MIGHT EVEN SAY IT'S...

...X-TRA GOOD!
SNIKT!
SNIKT!

OOOO-KAY.
AAAAAY..., YOU DOUBLE-DIPPED! AND THAT AIN'T COOL!

...SO THEN WE FIGURED OUT THE ISLAND WAS ALIVE AND, WELL, ACTUALLY, *I* FIGURED IT OUT AND...
AM I IN THE WRONG STRIP?
KNOCK! KNOCK! KNOCK!

HI, I'M THE FALCON! I'M HERE TO JOIN THE X-MEN!
...WHAT?

WAY BACK IN SOME FORGOTTEN CREVICE OF MARVEL CONTINUITY, IT WAS SUGGESTED THAT MY *TELEPATHIC LINK* WITH REDWING HERE WAS A *MUTANT POWER!* SO HERE I AM!

ZZZARRRKKK!!

NOW YOUR POWER SUCKS.

WHOA... YOUR BUDDY JUST FRIED THAT GUY'S BIRD!
YOU MIGHT EVEN SAY IT'S...
...X-TRA CRISPY!
SNIKT!
SNIKT!

KURT, WOULD YOU BE A DEAR AND GET ME A SLICE OF CAKE?
JA, MEIN FRAULEIN!

WHEW! NO MORE BROCCOLI FOR HIM!
I HOPE TO GOD THAT WASN'T GALACTUS.
BAMF!

HULK SEE CAKE. HULK EAT CAKE. THAT ALL THERE IS TO IT.

BAMF!

GOTT IN HIMELLLL...

OH, NO, THIS ONE NOT HULK'S FAULT THIS TIME! HULK JUST WANTED CAKE. THAT SO WRONG?

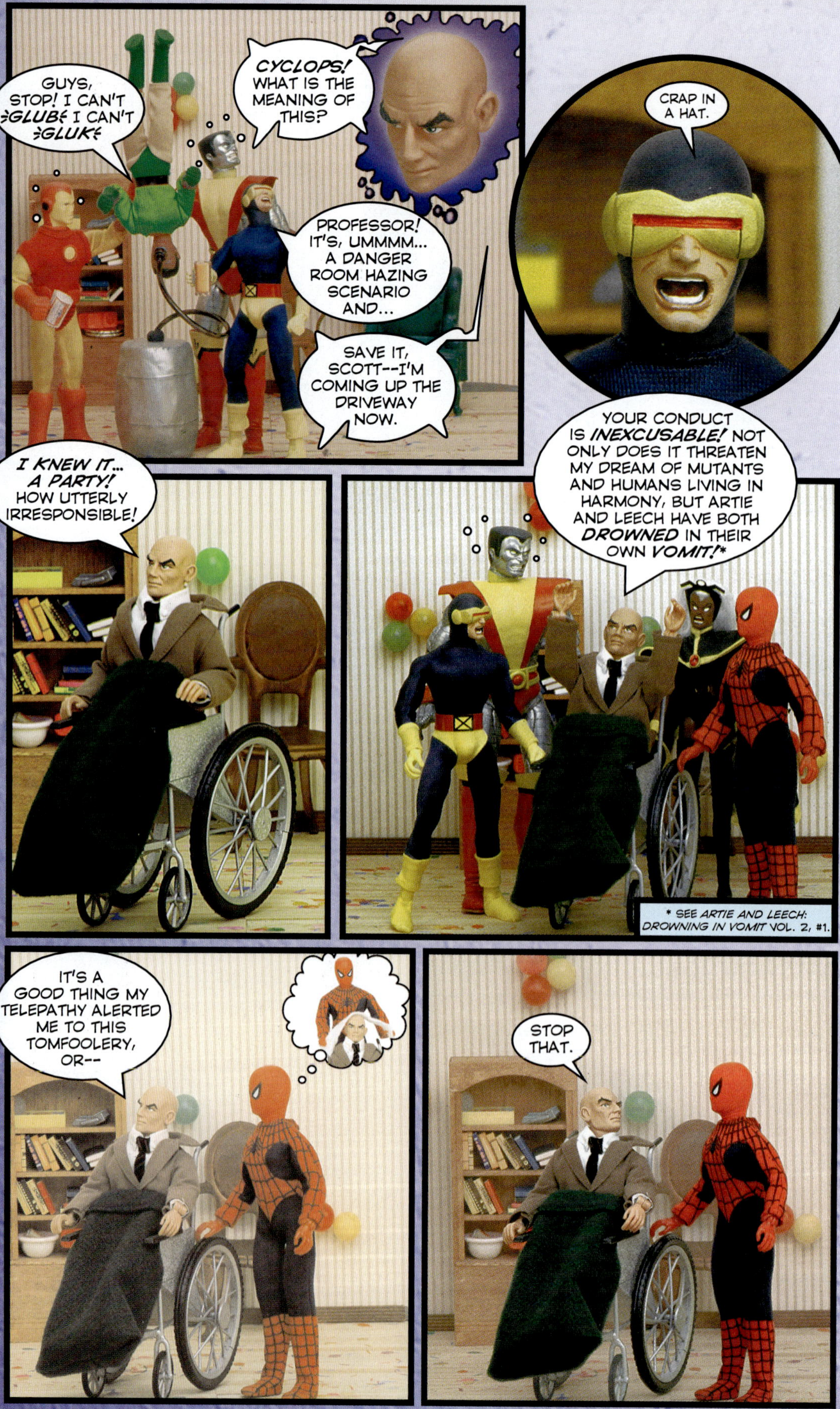

GUYS, STOP! I CAN'T ≶GLUB≶ I CAN'T ≶GLUK≶

CYCLOPS! WHAT IS THE MEANING OF THIS?

PROFESSOR! IT'S, UMMMM... A DANGER ROOM HAZING SCENARIO AND...

SAVE IT, SCOTT--I'M COMING UP THE DRIVEWAY NOW.

CRAP IN A HAT.

I KNEW IT... A PARTY! HOW UTTERLY IRRESPONSIBLE!

YOUR CONDUCT IS ***INEXCUSABLE!*** NOT ONLY DOES IT THREATEN MY DREAM OF MUTANTS AND HUMANS LIVING IN HARMONY, BUT ARTIE AND LEECH HAVE BOTH ***DROWNED*** IN THEIR OWN ***VOMIT!****

* SEE *ARTIE AND LEECH: DROWNING IN VOMIT* VOL. 2, #1.

THAT DOES IT! I'M CALLING ALL OF YOUR PARENTS, AND--
CAPTAIN! WE HAD FEARED WE WOULD NEVER FIND YOU! COME QUICKLY, RIKER HAS GONE MAD AND EATEN WESLEY!
WHAT THE HELL?

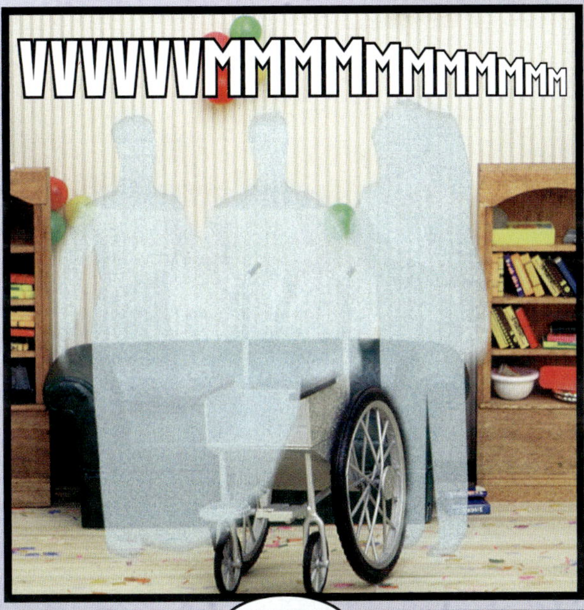
VVVVVVMMMMMMMMMMM

EITHER I'M GOING INSANE, OR...WELL, ACTUALLY I DON'T CARE EITHER WAY. THERE'S A KEG TO EMPTY.

LET'S MAKE THAT KEG...
X-TRA EMPTY!
SNIKT. SNIKT.

MUNCH! MUNCH! MUNCH!

NO WONDER HUMANITY HATES YOU GUYS.
SOB!
THE END

FALCON

Height: 8 inches
Weight: 2.4 oz.
Doesn't Mind: A little bird crap on his shoulder
First Appearance: "Clash of the Titans," *ToyFare* #8
Died: "A Few Good Megos," *ToyFare* #43
Died: "Viva Mego!" *ToyFare* #33
Died: "'Til Death Do You Part," *ToyFare* #57
Died: "I Am Legend, Part One," *ToyFare* #84
History: No one has the heart to tell the Falcon that his eponymous sidekick—Redwing the Falcon—clearly isn't a falcon. He looks more like a marshmallow Peep spray-painted red. Still, the Falcon (not "the Black Falcon," as he's known to Captain America [*ToyFare* #86]) is a valuable Avenger. When the leaves need to be raked out of the mansion's gutters, Falcon is there (*ToyFare* #45)! When you need a partner for a vaguely racist, two-man vaudeville act, Falcon is there (*ToyFare* #67)! Many have claimed that Falcon's origin involves him hatching out of a giant bird egg (*ToyFare* #64), but that's just not so. In truth, well, we think a bird bit him on the ass or something, giving him...a telekinetic link with winged rats? Actually, hatching out of an egg is much less depressing, so let's go with that origin.

The highlight of Falcon's superhero life (besides appearing in the direct-to-DVD smash *The Falcon & the Snowman* in *ToyFare* #58) was becoming President of the United States (*ToyFare* #70). Please, nobody tell him we just needed a black president for the *24* parody, and our go-to guy—Black Goliath—was out of town.
Known Relatives: The Falcon's "Secret Wars" counterpart first appeared in *ToyFare* #84 and was quickly torn limb from limb by the Marvel Legends gang.

TOYFARE #84 "I Am Legend, Part 1"

TOYFARE #86 "Heroes For Fired"

Twenty, Twenty, 24 Hours To Go

As originally published in *ToyFare* #70

"We rarely laughed as hard in our writers' meetings as we did when we came up with the Electro bit where every member of his family would be wearing an Electro mask."

- Tom Root

"I honestly think that at one point we were going to attempt to make this strip unfold in real-time just like *24*, but you can see for yourself how long that lasted. Also, and I probably don't need to point this out, Steve Irwin was still alive when we wrote this."

- Justin Aclin

THE FOLLOWING TAKES PLACE BETWEEN PAGES 106 AND 111. EVENTS HAPPEN IN REAL TIME.

BY: McCALLUM, ROOT & OAT

WITH: ACLIN, BRICKEN, PATYK & GUTIERREZ

EDITORS: SENREICH & GOLDSTEIN

DAMMIT, FURY--EVEN WITH THE COLOSTOMY BAG YOU'RE STILL THE BEST AGENT WE'VE GOT!
WHY CAN'T YOU HANDLE THIS?
IT'S...IT'S THE SYPHILIS, SIR.
TURNS OUT THAT GUY I THOUGHT WAS A CHICK GAVE IT TO ME BAD. I ONLY HAVE HOURS TO LIVE.

THAT LEAVES ONLY ONE MAN WHO CAN SAVE US. LEMME JUST DIAL DOWN THE CENTER AND...
Y'ELLO?

"MY NAME IS SPECIAL AGENT CAPTAIN AMERICA."
"A NUCLEAR BOMB HAS BEEN PLANTED SOMEWHERE IN MEGOVILLE."
"TODAY WILL BE THE LONGEST SIX PAGES OF MY LIFE."

SHORTLY*...
ALL RIGHT, ELECTRO...TALK!
EVERYONE WHO'S READ THE 'FALCON' MINI-SERIES KNOWS YOU'RE HIS ARCH-NEMESIS! WHERE'D YOU PLANT THE BOMB!?
...THE FALCON HAD HIS OWN SERIES?
BULLSH@#.
*YEAH, TRYING TO DO THIS IN REAL TIME WAS HARDER THAN WE THOUGHT.

WOULDYA LOOK AT THAT! AND THERE'S ME!
AND IS THAT REAGAN?*
FALCON
*YEP, THIS SERIES HAD THE FALCON, ELECTRO AND RONALD REAGAN! WHAT ARE YOU WAITING FOR? GO BUY IT.

ENOUGH TALK, ELECTRO! NOW TALK.
THESE ARE CLOSED-CIRCUIT MONITORS...EITHER YOU TELL ME WHERE THE BOMB IS OR YOU CAN WATCH YOUR FAMILY DIE ONE-BY-ONE!
CAN YOU MOVE MY CHAIR? I'M GETTING A GLARE FROM THE WINDOW.

"WE'LL START WITH YOUR WIFE!"
MY ONLY REGRET IS THAT I MARRIED ELECTROOOO--
BLAM!

TWO THINGS: FIRST OFF, THAT WASN'T MY WIFE. THAT WAS MY *EX*-WIFE.
SECOND, THAT WAS *AWESOME!*

YOU JUST SAVED ME LIKE THIRTY GRAND IN ALIMONY.
THE GUY YOU NEED TO TALK TO IS *KRAVEN*. HE'S A COMMIE.
AND D'YA THINK I CAN GET A COPY OF THAT TAPE?

HELLO, *BUCKY?* LISTEN CAREFULLY: YOU'VE GOT TO GET *OUT* OF MEGOVILLE. THERE'S A NUCLEAR BOMB SET TO GO OFF!
A *BOMB?!?* OHMIGODOHMIGOD OHMIGOD!

WE CAN'T HAVE A PANIC, SO TELL NO ONE! CAP OUT.

EH?
BUZZZZ!

OHMIGODOHMIGOD OHMIGOD! THERE'S A *BOMB* IN MEGOVILLE! GET OUT WHILE YOU CAN!
BUCKY, IT'S ME. YOU HIT THE WRONG SPEED DIAL.
...UMM, QUE?

LATER...
NUCLEAR BOMB? MMM...NOPE, DOESN'T RING ANY BELLS.
C'MON, IT'S ME, THE *CHAMELEON!* WE USED TO HANG TOGETHER IN THE LEGION OF DOOM!

TO PROVE YOU CAN TRUST ME, I'VE BROUGHT YOU THE HEAD OF YOUR SWORN ENEMY!
WHAT? I HAVE NO PROBLEM WITH THE GOBLIN.

OH...UH, HOW ABOUT HIM THEN?
HEY, HOW'SSS IT GOIN'?
NOPE.

HIM?
HE OWED ME FIFTY BUCKS!

AND HIM?
BINGO!
THE LAST LAUGH IS *MINE, IRWIN!*

I DON'T KNOW ANYTHING ABOUT A *NUCLEAR* BOMB, BUT I PLANTED A *REGULAR* BOMB AT AVENGERS MANSION.
D-MAN HAS TO GO.

DON'T EVEN THINK ABOUT IT.
MUNCH
MUNCH
Goldfish
I DON'T WANT ANYTHING TO DO WITH THIS STRIP.
12:27:33
THERE'S A *BOMB*, FROSTED FLAKES GUY!
GRRRR...
DAMMIT, MAN, IT'S LIKE PISSING *RAZOR BLADES!*

IRON MAN! GET OUT OF THE MANSION...THERE'S A BOMB!
URP
NO, MAN-- YOU DA' BOMB!
NO! YOU DON'T UNDERSTAND!
THERE'S A BOMB IN AVENGERS MANSION! YOU'VE GOT TO GET EVERYONE OUT BEFORE--
BOOM!

...I'M ON IT.

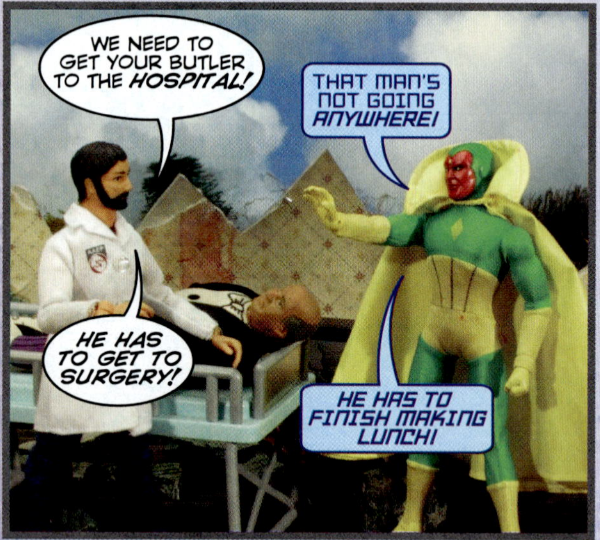
WE NEED TO GET YOUR BUTLER TO THE HOSPITAL!
THAT MAN'S NOT GOING ANYWHERE!
HE HAS TO GET TO SURGERY!
HE HAS TO FINISH MAKING LUNCH!

SKULL, YOU'VE GOT TO LISTEN! THERE'S A BOMB, HERE IN MEGOVILLE!
WELL, JA, I TIED YOU TO IT.

IT'S HOPELESS, MR. PRESIDENT. I EVEN LOOKED INSIDE MAN-THING.
DAMMIT... I KNEW I SHOULDA WENT WITH SOMEONE WHOSE CHEST STICKER WASN'T PEELING!

SUDDENLY...
SLAM!
WHO THE...?!
IT'S YOUR SIDEKICK, REDWING!
AND HE'S GOT THE NUCLEAR DETONATOR!

TWEET! TWEET! TWEET!*
*"CAP, YOU DON'T UNDERSTAND! THE FALCON IS REALLY AN EVIL SKRULL, AND SO IS HALF THE TOWN! THEY'VE BEEN INFILTRATING MEGOVILLE AND USING IT TO STAGE A GLOBAL INVASION! THE BOMB IS OUR ONLY HOPE OF STOPPING THEM!"

...WHAT'D HE SAY?
HE SAID YO' MOMMA'S A HO, AND SHE LIKE IT NASTY!

MY MOTHER WAS A SAINT!
SMISH!

MEANWHILE...
THIS DAY JUST SUCKS!
AND HOW DID I GET SYPHILIS?

S.H.I.E.L.D.
WINK!
FIGHTING FOR A BETTER TOMORROW!
END

ELECTRO

Height: 8.75 inches
Weight: 3.2 oz.
First Appearance (Pre-Crisis): "Idol Hands," *ToyFare* #67
First Appearance (Post-Crisis): "Have a Nice Day," *ToyFare* #10
Group Affiliation: The Sinister Six, the 'Lectric City Dance Troupe, Webelos
Died: "A Lizard In Every Pot," *ToyFare* #68
Died: "If This Be My Roast!" *ToyFare* #83
Died: "I Am Legend, Part One," *ToyFare* #84
History: Electro, like most of the so-called "supervillains" in Megoville, is a far more affable and pleasant fellow than any of the so-called "superheroes." In Post-Crisis continuity he was first glimpsed with his best friends, the misnomered "Sinister Six," razzing Dr. Doom. He later joined Venom, Kraven the Hunter and the Lizard, playing lead guitar in a KISS cover band ("Idol Hands," *ToyFare* #67). Electro has a long history of seeking to be the center of attention, including starring in a sitcom in an alternate reality (*ToyFare* #87) and attempting to deflect attention from Mysterio's stunts by breakdancing (*ToyFare* #81). His self-esteem issues are so great that he actually forced his family—including his ex-wife—to wear lightning-shaped masks. Why would Electro's ex-wife continue to wear an Electro mask? It was part of the twisted divorce settlement, which also required her to do the Electric Slide with the kids every other weekend. Electro's a dick like that.
Powers: Electro is possessed of electrical powers, which he's never actually been seen using in these pages, except to electrocute himself when he gets wet.

TOYFARE #68 "A Lizard in Every Pot"

TOYFARE #81 "Dome and Domer"

DEFENDERS ASSEMBLE

As originally published in *ToyFare* #47

"Violence against cats is just funny. They're so smug and self-righteous that when they end up in the Quaarog Dimension of Xevos you can't help but laugh. [*Editor's note: Tom is being sarcastic. Do not commit violence against cats.*] Violence against John Denver is also funny. At least it would have been if that wasn't just a Bo Duke Mego wearing the glasses off a George Burns doll."

- Tom Root

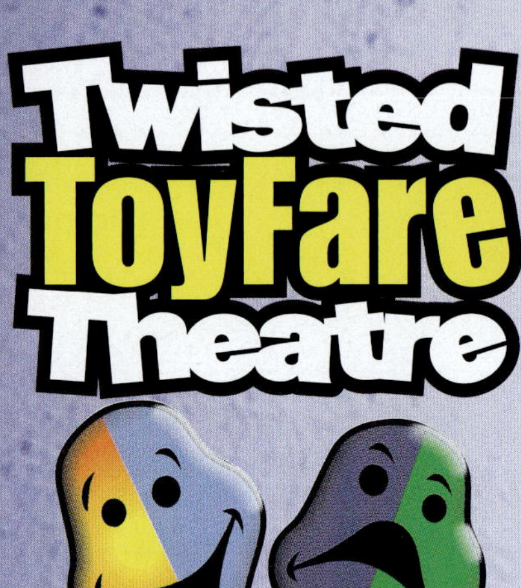

presents

DEFENDERS ASSEMBLE!

By Pat McCallum, Tom Root, Doug Goldstein and Bill Jensen

I'M FIVE HOURS LATE AND I'M NUMBER *THREE?* THE DEFENDERS ARE IN BIGGER TROUBLE THAN I THOUGHT.
DEFENDERS? THEN THE NECROPHILIAC HELP GROUP MUST BE *NEXT* DOOR!
3

SOON...
HELLO, APPLICANTS! I'M *DR. STRANGE!*
I'VE REVIEWED YOUR PAPERWORK, AND I'M AFRAID WE CAN ONLY ACCEPT *ONE* OF YOU TODAY!

PROVIDING YOUR OWN TRANSPORTATION IS VERY IMPORTANT!
MAN-THING, SINCE YOU CAN'T USE THE STATION WAGON IF YOUR MOTHER NEEDS IT, I'M AFRAID WE'RE GOING TO HAVE TO PASS ON YOU.

WELCOME TO THE *DEFENDERS,* SPIDER-MAN. *HOPE YOU SURVIVE* THE *EXPERIENCE!**
MY FREE GIFT IS A FOOTBALL PHONE?
RARRGH...
PHONE MADE IN CHILE. SOMETIMES FIRE HAZARD.
AND THEY'RE NOT WATERPROOF.
*"WELCOME TO (TITLE), (CHARACTER)! HOPE YOU SURVIVE THE EXPERIENCE!" IS ™ AND © MARVEL ENTERTAINMENT GROUP.

STILL LATER...
GATHER 'ROUND, DEFENDERS! TIME TO TAKE OUR SACRED DEFENDER OATH!

'IN BRIGHTEST DAY, IN BLACKEST NIGHT--'
WHOA, WHOA! I'M PRETTY SURE THAT'S A LAWSUIT WAITING TO HAPPEN!

THAT'S OKAY. WE CAN NEVER REMEMBER THE REST.
ON TO THE RUMPUS ROOM!
RUMPUS! RUMPUS! RUMPUS!

STILL, STILL LATER...
LOOK, IF YOU GUYS AREN'T GONNA DO ANYTHING, I'M HEADING HOME.
SORRY, SPIDER-MAN. THE FOOTBALL PHONE IS A LEGALLY BINDING CONTRACT.
WHAT? THERE'S NO ATLANTIS IN 'RISK'?
A POX ON YOU, MILTON BRADLEY!
GUYS... I SEE TROUBLE ON THE OFFICIAL DEFENDERS CRIMEPUTER!*
TROUBLE!
CHECKMATE! SOMEONE KING HULK.
*CNN.COM

AN INNOCENT LIFE HANGS IN THE BALANCE...
...AND EVERY SECOND COUNTS!

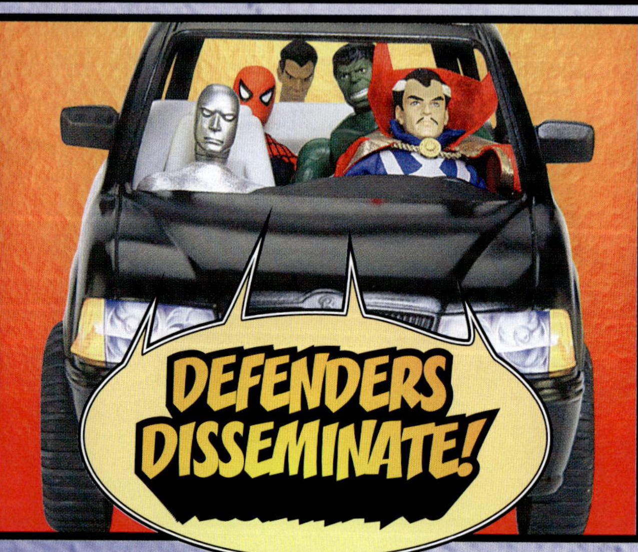
DEFENDERS DISSEMINATE!

MEW?
THIS IS THE INNOCENT LIFE? SOMEONE GET ME A ROCK.
NONSENSE, SPIDER-MAN! EVERY LIFE IS PRECIOUS...THAT'S THE DEFENDERS CREDO!*
*ACTUALLY, IT'S "EVERY LIFE IS PRECIOUS...EXCEPT THE FRENCH."

DEFENDERS...ARE...GO!!!
SERIOUSLY, JUST GET ME A ROCK.

HULK AND NAMOR, USE YOUR SUPER-STRENGTH TO SHAKE THE TREE AND KEEP MR. WHISKERS OFF-BALANCE!
WRETCHED SURFACE SHRUBBERY!
RAAAARGH!

MEANWHILE, THE SILVER SURFER WILL STUN THE BEAST WITH BLASTS HARNESSED FROM THE COSMIC POWER!
YES... THE, AH, "POWER COSMIC."

FINALLY, I, THE SORCERER SUPREME, SHALL OPEN A PORTAL TO--HEY LOOK, THERE'S ME!

MEW?

SO, HOW WAS THAT SAVING THE CAT?
IT'S OUT OF THE TREE, ISN'T IT?

IN THE QUAAROG DIMENSION OF XEVOS...
MEW?

MEANWHILE, DISASTER BREWS OVER COLORADO...
ROCKY MOUNTAIN HIGH!
THE CONTROLS ARE DEAD. I'M LOSING ALTITUDE!

COULD THIS BE THE END OF JOHN DENVER?
ONLY ONE CHANCE...

YOUNGBLOOD
FANTASTIC FOUR
DEFENDERS
MUST CHOOSE WISELY!

AT THAT VERY MOMENT...
THE ALERT! THERE'S TROUBLE IN COLORADO!
COLORADO? PFFT!
SOMEONE DOESN'T KNOW THE MEANING OF THE WORDS 'GAS BUDGET'!
RUMPUS! RUMPUS! RUMPUS!

LATER, BACK AT DEFENDERS HQ...
...I REPEAT, THIS IS AN INTERGALACTIC THREAT! THE FANTASTIC FOUR, AVENGERS AND X-MEN HAVE ALL ANSWERED THE CALL TO ARMS!

IF ANY OTHER HEROES ARE WATCHING, WE NEED YOUR HELP!
IN OTHER NEWS, BELOVED MUSICIAN JOHN DENVER MET WITH A TRAGIC--
THIS IS IT! THE CHANCE WE'VE BEEN WAITING FOR!

DEFENDERS ...ARE...!
SIGH
GO.

HOURS LATER, AT AVENGERS MANSION...
WHEW! THAT INTERGALACTIC THREAT WAS VERY NEARLY THE END OF THE AVEN--

WE... WE'VE BEEN ROBBED!
MY 'TOYFARE' COLLECTION... GONE!*
*SEE? VISION BUYS "TOYFARE" AND SO SHOULD YOU!

DEFENDERS HQ...
RARRGH! HELMET SAY MILK IN FRIDGE GO BAD.
I'LL TRADE YOU THAT CEREBRO HELMET FOR THIS BEER-FILLED ARMOR.
SHUDDER
YOU, JARVIS! MAKE WITH THE FOOT MASSAGE!
WE'RE GOING TO MAKE A KILLING ON EBAY THE LIKES OF WHICH THE WORLD HAS NEVER SEEN!
GREAT. I'LL THROW IN MY FOOTBALL PHONE.
END

MAN-THING

Height: 9 inches
Weight: 19.1 oz.
Occupation: Guardian of Nexus of All Realities, punchline to countless "Giant-Size Man-Thing" jokes
First Appearance: "Working for the Man," *ToyFare* #31
Died: "Viva Mego!" *ToyFare* #33
Died: "'Til Death Do You Part," *ToyFare* #57
Died: "I Am Legend, PartTwo," *ToyFare* #85
Died: "Someone on This Cover Dies," *ToyFare* #100
History: Man-Thing is a muck monster of few-to-no words and one of the only Megoville inhabitants who speaks only in crude symbols. This inability to communicate trumps his ability to burn people to death with his touch and has cost him a coveted spot in Dr. Strange's Defenders team (*ToyFare* #47). Career lowlights include accidentally burning Franklin Richards into a pile of ashes (*ToyFare* #38). Highlights include hitting a ground double in the Mego Superheroes: Secret Wars contest of champions (*ToyFare* #60). The perpetually lonely creature has a sole ally in Mego Alan Moore, who inexplicably sticks up for him every chance he gets, going into a violent rage if someone compares Man-Thing to Swamp Thing. When Moore appeared on a motorcycle, saving Man-Thing's ass at the last second ("I Am Legend, Part 1," *ToyFare* #84), the tomato-eyed pile of goop discovered what true love really meant.

Man-Thing was last seen hurtling towards the sun when Dr. Doom launched Spider-Man's house into orbit.

Powers: Whoever knows fear burns at the touch of the Man-Thing. Whoever knows fear and is covered in gasoline burns twice as fast.

TOYFARE #38 "Hit Me Baby One More Time"

TOYFARE #100 "Someone On This Cover Dies"

28 Smurfs Later

As originally published in *ToyFare* #76

"Smurf brain matter is apparently blue clay. The panel at the end, imploring kids to 'Live the movie!' by eating Smurf Magic Berries cereal, is still one of my favorites. And I loved the birds-eye view of Papa Smurf about to get zombie goo dripped into his eye. *28 Days Later* was one of those movies that sticks with you for a long time after you see it, and writing a parody of it with Smurfs was pretty delightful."

- Tom Root

Twisted
ToyFare
Theatre
PRESENTS
28
SMURFS
LATER
BY:
McCALLUM,
ROOT
& OAT
WITH:
ACLIN,
PATYK,
GUTIERREZ,
SENREICH &
GOLDSTEIN

WITH THIS SPECIAL *FERTILIZER* I MADE, I CAN MAKE THE SMURFBERRY CROP *BIGGER* AND *SMURFIER!*
I'LL *FINALLY* GET THE RESPECT I DESERVE FROM THE OTHER SMURFS!

OF COURSE, I *COULD* SMURF THE SAME THING IF I STOPPED ACTING LIKE SUCH AN INSUFFERABLE A-HOLE, BUT I'D RATHER DO IT THROUGH *SCIENCE!*

NOW TO LET THE FERTILIZER SOAK IN, AND IN A WEEK THEY'LL BE JUST *SMURFY!*

SECONDS LATER...
THESE SMURFBERRIES LOOK *PERFECT* FOR MY FAMOUS SMURFBERRY PIES!
PLUS, THEY'LL DISGUISE THE TASTE OF DRIFTER SMURF!

SOON...
MMM, EATING A WARM, MOIST SMURFBERRY SLICE IS THE *SECOND* SMURFIEST THING TO DO WITH A PIE!
YOU JUST GOTTA DO 'EM IN THE RIGHT ORDER!
SLURP!
CHOMP!
CHOMP!
MMM
I CAN TASTE *ME!*

I...I DON'T FEEL SO SMUR... SMUR...
RHARGHHHH!
HUUUURRRRK!
SAY IT, DON'T SMUR... SMUR...
RHARGHHHH!

ZOMBIES!
F'N ZOMBIES!
WE SHOULD NEVER HAVE FORSAKEN JESUS!
BRAINS! BRAINS!

HU-YUCK, YUCK, YUCK!
JOKEY!
WE'VE GOT TO...TO...IS THAT SMURF FOR ME?
AW, YOU SHOULDN'T HAVE!
BLAM!
...YOU A-HOLE.
WE COULD HAVE USED THAT TO FIGHT THE ZOMBIES!
BRAINS!

HEFTY!
BUT...BUT YOU'RE NOT EVEN A ZOMBIE!
HEY, PROTEIN'S PROTEIN.
CHOMP!
SLURP!
ONE SIDE!
I CAME HERE TO KICK SMURF AND CHEW BUBBLESMURF...
SHOVE!
JOSTLE!

...AND I'M ALL OUT OF BUBBLESMURF!
IF THESE ZOMBIES ARE LOOKING FOR TROUBLE, I'VE GOT THE MAP!
THIS WAY, SMURFS!
SOK!

I HAVE A SMURFY IDEA... WE CAN HIDE UNDERWATER.
NO, YOU FOOL!
MY GOD... THE SNORKS ARE CONTAMINATED, TOO!
NO, THEY'RE JUST PISSED THEIR CARTOON SUCKED.

ARE WE THERE YET?
NO.
ARE WE THERE YET?
NO.
ARE WE THERE YET?
NO!
ARE WE--
SMURF ME THAT ONE MORE TIME, *BEE-YOTCH!*
SMACK!

WE CAN SMURF UNDER THIS TREE UNTIL WE CATCH OUR BREATH.
...DOES 'SMURF' MEAN 'REST'?
I HOPE NOT!
TEE-HEE!
WE'LL MOVE ON AT FIRST--EH?
POIT!
MY EYE!

SMURF AWAY! SMURF A...*A*...
RHARGHHHH!
BLAM!
...OOK?

YOU SAVED US FROM THE ZOMBIE PAPA SMURF!
HE WAS A ZOMBIE?*
*NOBODY SHOW THIS PANEL TO MATT GROENING.
MEANWHILE...
OH, NO!
AZRAEL'S GONE *RABID* FROM EATING THOSE WRETCHED SMURFS!
MRROW NROW

SOB!
GOODBYE, MY ONLY FRIEND!
BLAM!

SOON...
RRRRRUMBLE!
PET SEMATERY
MS. LION R.I.P
AZRAEL

KRA-KOOM!
AZRAEL

BOOM!
AZRAEL

I DON'T THINK HE'S COMING BACK.
AZRAEL

AT THAT MOMENT, EVEN THOUGH IT'S APPARENTLY DAYLIGHT NOW...*
ARMY BASE
LOOK!
WE'RE SAVED, SMURFETTE!
*WEIRD, RIGHT? IT WAS NIGHTTIME A PANEL AGO.**
** YEAH, THAT IS WEIRD. DO THE EDITORS OF THIS MAG EVEN TAKE THE TIME TO READ THIS CRAP?***
*** YO, BACK OFF. THAT MAP THING ON PAGE 254 DOESN'T WRITE ITSELF. BESIDES, NO ONE'S GONNA NOTICE.
BUDDA
BUDDA
BUDDA
BASE
WE MADE IT!
HOORAY FOR DEUS EX MACHINA!
POK
SPURT
SMAT

WELL, THE GOOD NEWS IS YOU'RE SAFE FROM THE ZOMBIES.
THE BAD NEWS IS I PROMISED MY SMURFS SOME WOMEN.
PANT
PANT
EH, I CAN LIVE WITH... SMURFETTE!
SMASH!
EEEEEEE!
BRAINS!

WELL, I GUESS WE'RE JUST GONNA HAVE TO MAKE DO...
SON OF A BITCH.
PANT
PANT
PANT
PANT
HEY, KIDS!
Post
SMURF
MAGIC
BERRIES
INSIDE
GUMMI
GOODIES
LIVE
THE
MOVIE!
END

GARGAMEL

Height: 8 inches
Weight: 1.8 oz.
Occupation: Fascist Anti-Smurf Wizard
Known Associates: Azrael the cat...actually, that's about it
Favorite *Risk* Strategy: Always starts off going after South America
First Appearance: "28 Smurfs Later," *ToyFare* #76
History: Gargamel must have been Smurfed up the Smurf with hot Smurfberry acid, because we can't think of another reason for this hang-toothed old geezer to hate a blue-skinned race of pixies so much. What's that? Smurfs can be used to create gold? So why does Gargamel wear the same black, cheapass robe every day? Simply put, the Trix Rabbit gets more cereal than Gargamel kills Smurfs, which is why his victory over "Calcium Deficient Smurf" (who was captured by net after shattering his knee) is so notable. He reveals this "chewy blue" victory to Cobra Commander, Megatron and Skeletor at their Wednesday board game night (*ToyFare* #82) and details how eating the blue bugger had him tripping balls all night long. Gargamel's greatest personal tragedy came when he shot his longtime cat-companion, Azrael, after the nasty bastard became an even-nastier rabid zombie (*ToyFare* #76). However, the wretched cat eventually came back, crapping pointy Micronauts villain Baron Karza into his litter box. He hasn't walked straight since.
Arsenal: A federal raid of Gargamel's low-income forest shack found several illegal Wizard Tomes, nets dipped in formaldehyde, large quantities of the hallucinogen "Peyo-te" and illicit recipes for a "human-sized Smurfette." He was charged with premeditated Smurficide and intent to exploit a nationally protected fantasy creature.

***TOYFARE* #82** "Risky Business"

***TOYFARE* #82** "Risky Business"

Nobody Does It Vader

As originally published in *ToyFare* #93

"The original pitch was four different Jedi going off to find Vader—but how do you tell four Jedis apart, give them individual personalities for the jokes and explain how they're not all dead by the time of the Original Trilogy? It was easier (and better) to just use different types of Stormtroopers and make them different kinds of dicks. And it worked—those four went on to be a big hit around the office, and our readers seem to like them, too."

- Jon Gutierrez

BY:
McCALLUM, OAT & ACLIN

WITH:
GUTIERREZ, KARDON & WARD

I GUESS WE SHOULD GO RESCUE HIM...KID, YOU STAY--GAH!
I'M NOT A KID, AND I'M TIRED OF YOU HOLDING ME BACK!
PIP-PIP!

MEANWHILE...
YOU WILL TELL ME THE SECRET OF THE GENESIS TORPEDO OR I WILL KILL ONE OF THE PRISONERS!
HA!
NEWS FLASH, JOHNNY FOREHEAD, I'M THE ONLY PRISONER!
WAITAMINUTE...

TAKE THAT!
AND THIS ONE'S FOR MY MOM!
DUDE, WHAT'D YOU DO TO HIS MO--URK!
ME?!?
I DIDN'T TOUCH HIS--HURK!

OH DEAR, I HOPE MY HEAD CAN KLINGON HERE AWHILE!
THIS BATTLE IS CERTAINLY NECK AND NECK!
SLICE
PLOP

SERIOUSLY... WHY DID VADER BUILD SUCH A GAY ROBOT?
I JUST WANNA GET A TAPE OF WHAT THE KLINGONS DID TO HIS MOM.
R-R-RUMBLE!

R-R-RUMBLE!
BACK TO THE SHIP— THE PLANET'S COLLAPSING!
JUST LIKE THE STAR TREK FRANCHISE!
ZING!

I'LL JUST KLINGON HERE...
YOU ALREADY USED THAT PUN!

YOU DON'T HAVE TO GET SO MAD A-BOOT IT.
GAH!
I AM SICK...
AND TIRED...
OF YOU!
KICK

DIDJA GET RID OF HIM?
MORE OR LESS.
I WISH I'D SEEN MORE BROADWAY PLAAAAYS...

WOW, I FEEL GREAT!
I'VE REACHED ADULTHOOD, AND I DON'T HAVE TO WEAR THAT UNCOMFORTABLE ARMOR TO HIDE MY HORRIBLE BURNS!
BOOM
S-SOME HOT C-C-COFFEE, MR. S-S-SKYWALKER?
SURE, SHAKEY PETE!

LATER...
...AND THAT'S WHAT HAPPENED BETWEEN EPISODES FOUR AND FIVE.
NOT THAT IT MATTERS, SINCE IT'S ALL NON-CANON.
YOU'RE ALL SO BRAVE, AND I LOVE A MAN IN A RUBBERMAID UNIFORM!
YEAH, ACING THAT ASSIGNMENT GOT US THIS SWEET GIG...

...RUNNING SECURITY HERE IS A SNAP!
ESPECIALLY NOW THAT THE WEAPON SYSTEMS ARE FULLY ARMED AND OPERATIONAL!

LET'S BLOW THIS DUMP AND THEN GO GET A ROOM.
...YOU ARE A CHICK, RIGHT?
GUH.
END

My Big Fat Fat Wedding

As originally published in *ToyFare* #79

"Even as a kid, I was disturbed by Doc Ock wanting to marry Aunt May in the comics. I thought about how awkward that would've been for Peter and how horrifying their eight-armed make out sessions would be."

- Jon Gutierrez

"This strip came about because we wanted to get a custom Doc Ock Mego made to use on our cover, and it was my job to liaise with customizer Bret Bolden to make sure Ock was fat and gross enough. Mission accomplished!"

- Justin Aclin

BY:
McCALLUM,
ROOT, OAT
& ACLIN

WITH:
PATYK,
GUTIERREZ,
SENREICH &
GOLDSTEIN

...
TIME FOR ME TO LEAVE THIS ISSUE'S STORY BEFORE I SEE SOMETHING *ELSE* I CAN'T UNSEE.

THERE'S GOTTA BE *SOMETHING* BETTER I CAN GET INVOLVED WITH THIS MONTH IF I JUST LOOK HARD ENOUGH.*
*NO CHANCE. THIS WHOLE MAGAZINE IS STUPID. —ED.

RHARGHHH!
SOMEBODY SAAAAAVE HULK...

OLD NAKED PEOPLE IT IS.

HEY, KID! *URP!* YOU'RE OUTTA PRINGLES.
AND FROM NOW ON CALL ME *'DAD'* ON ACCOUNT OF ME BANGIN' YOUR MOM.
SHE'S NOT MY MOM.
GOOD. I HATE KIDS.

NOW, SIDDOWN-- *NASCAR'S* ON AND I NEED SOMEONE TO RUB MY FAT.
OTTO

OH, IT'S THAT HORRIBLE SPIDER-MAN AGAIN!
OTTO AND I HAVE AN ANNOUNCEMENT TO MAKE!
HOPEFULLY, IT'S ABOUT A THREESOME WITH DR. KEVORKIAN.

WE'RE GETTING MARRIED!
YUP, IN VEGAS!
THAT WAY EVEN IF THE WEDDING NIGHT'S A BUST I CAN STILL GET LUCKY.

I WONDER IF I CAN CATCH UP WITH THE HULK...
HULK NOT CARE HOW YOU DO IT, JUST SAAAAAVE...
VEGAS IT IS.

THANK YOU FOR CHOOSING MEGOVILLE AIRLINES FOR YOUR FLIGHT TO LAS VEGAS!
NOW, FOR THE LAST TIME, PLEASE TURN OFF ALL ELECTRIC DEVICES.

...WHAT?

HELLO...?
HEY, MIDNIGHT RUN, HURRY IT UP IN THERE.
AVATORY
KNOCK
KNOCK

WOO!
SAY 'HELLO' TO THE TWO NEWEST MEMBERS OF THE MILE HIGH CLUB!
...GOOD CHRIST...
WE HAVEN'T TAKEN OFF YET.

THEN IT'S A GOOD THING I SWEAT BUTTER, 'CAUSE ROUND TWO'S GONNA BE NEEDIN' SOME LUBRICANT!
TORY
...THIS NEVER HAPPENS TO ULTIMATE ME.

THERE'S GOTTA BE A CRAPPER IN COACH I CAN--
WHOA.

I DIDN'T KNOW FAT KIDS NAMED 'OTTO' HAD THIS MANY FRIENDS.

!
WHAT THE...?!

SPIDER-MAN!

THAT MASKED MISCREANT...ON MY FLIGHT!
TIME FOR ANOTHER SCATHING EDITORIAL ABOUT HIM!
YOUR REAL NAME IS 'JONAH JONAH JAMESON'?

ALWAYS BET ON BLACK!
DER BOOK SAYS NOT ALWAYS.
HOW TO GAMBLE

PSSST! HEY, SPIDER-MAN!
CHECK THIS OUT...

EH-HEH-HEH-HEH...
EEK
EEK

WH-WHA...?
VMMMMM!

HA!
YOU WERE DRAWING ON YOUR FACE ALL ALONG!
MYSTERIO, MASTER OF ILLUSION, STRIKES AGAIN!

AND NOW, LIKE THE MORNING FOG RECEDING AT DAWN'S FIRST LIGHT, I VANISH!
PAMPF!

MWAH-HA-HA-HA!

SLAM!

FEH!
THE VULTURE HAS NO NEED FOR PEANUTS OR E-TICKETS!

A MAN... BY THE WING!

AND TOILET PAPER THESE DAYS IS TOO DAMN SOFT!
IN MY DAY, IF YOU WANTED A CLEAN TUCHUS, YOU'D--
GGRRMM...
WHAT THE?!

BZZZOWNT!

OH, MY GOD... STEWARDESS!
STEWARDESS!

YES?
HOW ABOUT YOU POUR US A BOURBON AND LOSE THE SKIRT?
CLINK
CLINK

SHORTLY, AT THE HOTEL...
I'M SSSO HUNGRY!
WANNA HIT THE BUFFET?

ENUFF!
KRAVEN WAITS IN BREAD LINE NEVER AGAIN!
I SHALL BE THE ONE FINDING US FOOD, DA?

EIGHT MINUTES LATER...
THIS ONE WANTED TO BE PETTED AND HAVE BELLY RUBBED.
DIG IN, TOVARISCH.
OH, BOY!

GLOM!

GAK!
HE'S CHOKING!

HANG ON, COMRADE!
KRAVEN SHALL SAVE YOU!
GURK!

PTOOO!
CRASH!

YOUR FIRST DAY HOME FROM THE HOSPITAL, ROY!
HOW DO YOU FEEL?
MMMMMMPHH.*
*"MAYBE WE TRAINS THE PUPPIES NOW, YES?"

ROY!
WHAM!
SMISH!

BAD KITTY.
TAP
TAP

MEANWHILE...
MYSTERIO, THE MASTER OF ILLUSION, IS TRAPPED...
...OR IS HE?!

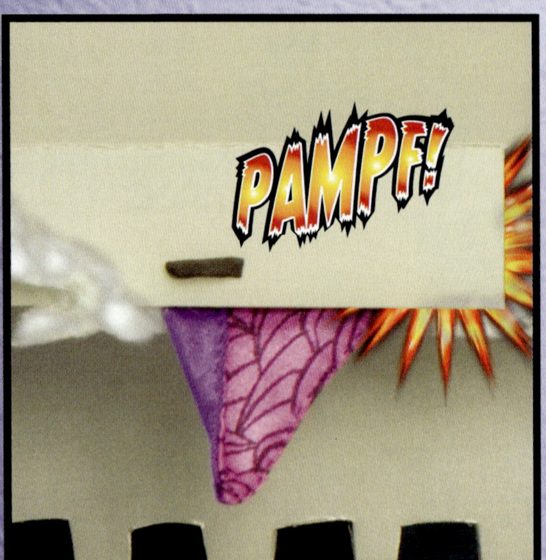
PAMPF!

COUGH
COUGH
...HELLO?

THE BIG DAY...
...AND WITH THE POWERS VESTED IN ME, MAMA, I NOW PRONOUNCE YOU MAN AND--

STOP THAT MAN!
BLAM!

HA, YOU DIDN'T EVEN BREAK THE *SKIN*. YOU--
ARGH!
MY... MY *HEART!*

HE HAD A HEART ATTACK... HE'S *DEAD!*
AND HIS POCKETS ARE FULL OF CAKE.
OTTO!

WHY DIDN'T YOU STOP HIM, SPIDER-GUY?
ALL YOU HAD TO DO WAS *TRIP* HIM AND YOU WOULD HAVE *SAVED* YOUR UNCLE OTTO.
HEY, THIS IS THE ONLY PART OF THE STORY I'M *COOL* WITH.
NOOOOOOO!
BUT...BUT I'M *PREGNANT* WITH HIS *CHILD!*

THAT'S GONNA BE ONE *DUSTY* BABY.

CLINK
END

MYSTERIO

Height: 8 inches
Weight: 4.4 oz.
Group Affiliation: The Sinister Six, Professional Stage Magicians Association
Known Relatives: Has a wife who also wears a fishbowl on her head and who cheated on him with Spider-Man
First Appearance (Pre Crisis): "My Big Fat Fat Wedding," *ToyFare* #79
First Appearance (Post-Crisis): "Have a Nice Day," *ToyFare* #10
Died: "Viva Mego!" *ToyFare* #33
Died: "If This Be My Roast!" *ToyFare* #83
Died: "I Am Legend, Part One," *ToyFare* #84
History: How sinister can a guy with a fishbowl on his head be? Sinister enough to be in the Sinister Six! Mysterio, the master of illusions, made his debut as a member of the notorious supervillain team known for terrorizing Spider-Man. Except that Mysterio is far more likely to be seen terrorizing his good friend and teammate Electro than Spidey. Mysterio's chief power is his ability to perform amazing illusions, which he chiefly uses for the purpose of cheap publicity, such as when he suspended himself in a glass case above Megoville for no particular reason (in *ToyFare* #81). Mysterio's crowning glory came in *ToyFare* #100 when, in the course of an evil-off contest, he and Electro executed a dine and dash on a really nice restaurant. He was last seen getting arrested when the police broke up a supervillain "Acts of Vengeance" convention in *ToyFare* #111. Don't worry, though, Mysterio will be back—he's fun to write!
Deadliest Weapon: The well-placed *bon mot*. See: "That's gonna be one dusty baby."
So...What's Under That Fishbowl? Fish, we assume.

TOYFARE #81 "Dome and Domer"

TOYFARE #100 "Someone On This Cover Dies"

The Daredevil's Advocate

As originally published in *ToyFare* #91

"Tom Root was a defining force on 'TTT' for so many years, and this was the first strip after he left. So it's the first time I was able to bully one of my ideas into completion pretty much as I had envisioned it. All credit to Zach Oat—this was also his first issue as storyboard artist, taking over for Tom—for pulling off the conceptually difficult (and ridiculous) 'self-cross-examination' sequence."

- Justin Aclin

Twisted ToyFare Theatre PRESENTS

The Daredevil's Advocate

BY: McCALLUM, OAT & ACLIN

WITH: GUTIERREZ, GOLDSTEIN & WARD

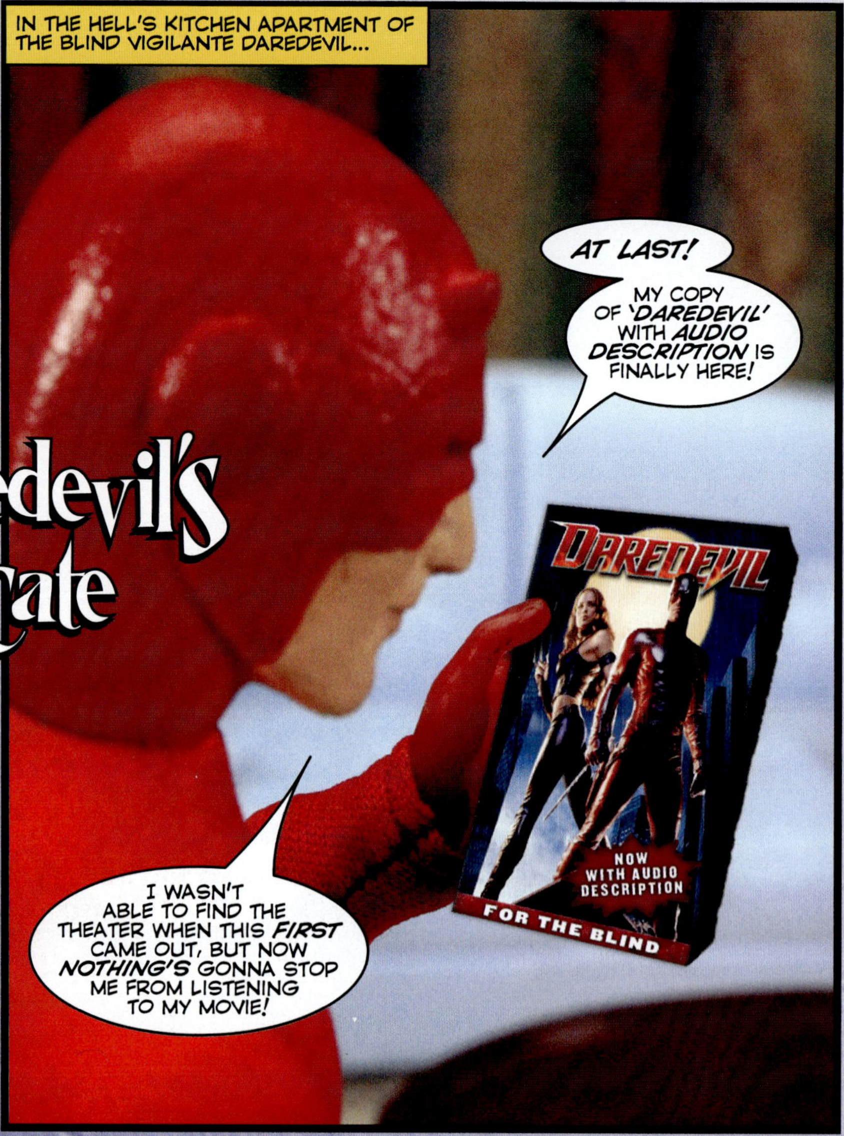

IN THE HELL'S KITCHEN APARTMENT OF THE BLIND VIGILANTE DAREDEVIL...

AT LAST!

MY COPY OF *'DAREDEVIL'* WITH *AUDIO DESCRIPTION* IS FINALLY HERE!

DAREDEVIL

NOW WITH AUDIO DESCRIPTION

FOR THE BLIND

I WASN'T ABLE TO FIND THE THEATER WHEN THIS *FIRST* CAME OUT, BUT NOW *NOTHING'S* GONNA STOP ME FROM LISTENING TO MY MOVIE!

AND THE FILM TRUDGES ON...
OKAY, THIS SCENE'S STRAIGHT OUT OF THE COMICS, EXCEPT BULLSEYE'S *IRISH*, *BALD* AND HAS THE *'TARGET' STORE* LOGO ON HIS FOREHEAD.
...WHAT?

...AND ON...
NOW WE MEET THE KINGPIN, WHO'S *BLACK*, UNLIKE THE COMIC VERSION, WHO'S WHITE.
WAIT, THE KINGPIN'S *NOT* BLACK?

...UNTIL...
NOW ELEKTRA IS FIGHTING MURDOCK ON A *SEE-SAW* AND-- YOU KNOW WHAT, I CAN'T TAKE ANY MORE. I QUIT.
THAT'S *IT!*
I'LL GET MY *JUSTICE* IN THE ONLY WAY A GRITTY, SPANDEX-CLAD VIGILANTE OF THE STREETS KNOWS *HOW*...

HEAR YE, HEAR YE!
THE COURT WILL NOW HEAR THE CASE OF *DAREDEVIL VS. BEN AFFLECK*, FOR THE CRIME OF EVERY MOVIE SINCE 'GOOD WILL HUNTING' AND THE *LESSER* CHARGE OF CHARACTER DEFAMATION!

REPRESENTING THE *PROSECUTION* WILL BE, UH...MATT MURDOCK.
YOUR ASS IS *MINE*, AFFLECK!

REPRESENTING THE DEFENSE WILL BE *JENNIFER WALTERS*.
I CAN PUT A 'BEN' IN YOUR 'NIFFER.'
NOT GONNA HAPPEN.

ALL RISE FOR THE HONORABLE JUDGE DAVE *QUINTESSON!*
GUILTY!
NOT YET, YOUR HONOR.

DOES THE JURY UNDERSTAND THEIR--
GUILTY!
NOT Y-- OH, LET'S JUST GET ON WITH IT.

AS MY FIRST WITNESS I CALL...*STAN LEE,* TRUE BELIEVER!
WOW, THAT *IS* FUN TO SAY.

MR. LEE, *DID* YOU OR DID YOU *NOT* SEE 'DAREDEVIL'?
IN THE *MIGHTY MARVEL* (AND NOW POW ENTERTAINMENT) *MANNER,* I--
BZZT!

WOOP, THERE GOES MY *SIGNAL WATCH!*
GOTTA RUN!

EXCELSIOR!
FWOOOSH!
CRASH!

GOODYEAR
ANSWER THE *QUESTION,* MR. LEE--IF THAT *IS* YOUR REAL NAME, WHICH I KNOW IT IS *NOT!*

BOOM!
...
I THOUGHT SO.
I'M *DONE* WITH THIS WITNESS, YOUR HONOR.

YOUR WITNESS, MS. WALTERS.
NO QUESTIONS FOR THE GUY WHO FLEW INTO THE BLIMP, YOUR HONOR.
I CALL TO THE STAND DAREDEVIL'S PORN-STAR JUNKIE EX-GIRLFRIEND... KAREN PAGE!

DO YOU SWEAR TO TELL THE TRUTH, THE WHOLE TRUTH AND NOTHING BUT THE TRUTH?
I'LL ████ YOUR ████ FOR A DOLLAR.

OBJECTION!
OVERRULED!
STENOGRAPHER, READ THAT BACK... BUT SLOWLY.

"NEXT I CALL TO THE STAND... THE AMAZING SPIDER-MAN!"
PSST, I'M REALLY DAREDEVIL.
YOU'RE TALKING INTO THE MICROPHONE.

OBJECTION!
THEY'RE YOUR QUESTIONS!
OVERRULED!
...WHAT?

MR. MAN, WHERE WERE YOU ON THE NIGHT OF FEBRUARY FIFTEENTH?
...THAT'S NEXT FRIDAY.
I KNOW... YOU BUSY?
YO, I READ THAT ISSUE OF X-MEN*, AND NO WAY I'M TAKING JUGGERNAUT'S SLOPPY SECONDS.
ONCE YOU GO JUGGERNAUT, IT'S PHYSICALLY IMPOSSIBLE TO GO BACK.
*'UNCANNY X-MEN' #435. NO, REALLY.

OBJECTION!
YOUR HONOR, I MOVE TO STRIKE ALL OF CHUCK AUSTEN'S WORK FROM CONTINUITY!
SUSTAINED.

VOO-HOO!
I DON'T SUCK ANYMORE!

THINGS ARE LOOKING GRIM... TIME FOR MATT MURDOCK TO CALL A SURPRISE WITNESS...
YOUR HONOR, I CALL TO THE STAND...
DAREDEVIL!
GASP!
SHOCK!

ZIS IS GOING TO BE FANTASTIK!

IF YOU'LL EXCUSE ME A MOMENT, I MUST STEP THROUGH THIS DOOR AND...UM, SEE IF I CAN FIND THE WITNESS.

NOW, IN THE SECRECY OF THIS BROOM CLOSET, I CAN CHANGE TO DAREDEVIL AND PULL OFF THE GREATEST RUSE IN LEGAL HISTORY!

DAREDEVIL, THE MAN WITHOUT FEAR IS HERE!
HEY! THAT RHYMED!
I SWEAR!
MR. DAREDEVIL, TELL THE COURT HOW YOU FELT WHEN YOU SAW THE 'DAREDEVIL' MOVIE!
CONFUSED, ANGRY...
...AND WHAT'S UP WITH JENNIFER GARNER'S JAWLINE?
AND HAS THIS MOVIE AFFECTED YOUR ROLE AS, LIKE, A TOTALLY COOL, STREET-TOUGH SUPERHERO?
YES, IT...IT... SOB!
STRONG MEN ALSO CRY, MR. MURDOCK... STRONG MEN ALSO CRY...
I REST MY CASE!
VUNDERBAR!
CLAP
CLAP
CLAP
ENOUGH!
I NOW RETIRE TO MY QUARTERS TO DELIBERATE AND WATCH THE DIRECTOR'S CUT OF 'REINDEER GAMES.'
GULP!

ONE HUNDRED AND TWENTY-FOUR MINUTES LATER...
ABOMINATION!
I RULE THAT BEN AFFLECK MUST PAY DAREDEVIL FORTY MILLION DOLLARS AND TAKE ACTING LESSONS!

BUT...BUT I NEVER LOSE A CASE!
I...I...
RHARGHH!
SHE-HULK SMASH!
RRRRIP!
YEAH, NOW RIP OFF THE BOTTOMS...

NO, WAIT, MY FACE, MY OSCAR-WINNING FA--
SQUARK!
SKREE-ONK!
AAAH!
AAAH!

WAIT, BEN AFFLECK'S A ROBOT?
YA, ALL ACTORS ARE ROBOTS...OR GAY.
OR GAY ROBOTS.
SMASH!
REND!
CLOBBER!

SUCCESS!
AND NOW WITH BEN AFFLECK'S HARD-EARNED MONEY, I CAN MAKE THE DAREDEVIL MOVIE THE WAY I WANT!
AIEEEE!
RUN FOR YOUR LIFE!

AND SO...
BUT I DON'T HAVE ANY MONEY! HOW WILL I PAY FOR THE PIZZA...?
I'LL FIGHT YOU FOR IT ON A SEE-SAW!
PIZZA
BA-CHIKKA-WA-WAA
END

Beach Blanket Mego

As originally published in *ToyFare* #24

"I'd put 'work the parapet' as one of the best things ever to appear in the pages of any Wizard product. I sure enjoyed making those Atlanteans. There's something inherently funny about adding top hats and canes to characters who don't normally use them."

- Tom Root

"It's definitely not one of my favorites, because I always thought that the invasion by the Atlanteans would be funnier. In hindsight I don't know what you could do with these blue fish people. So maybe that's the best we could have come up with."

- Doug Goldstein

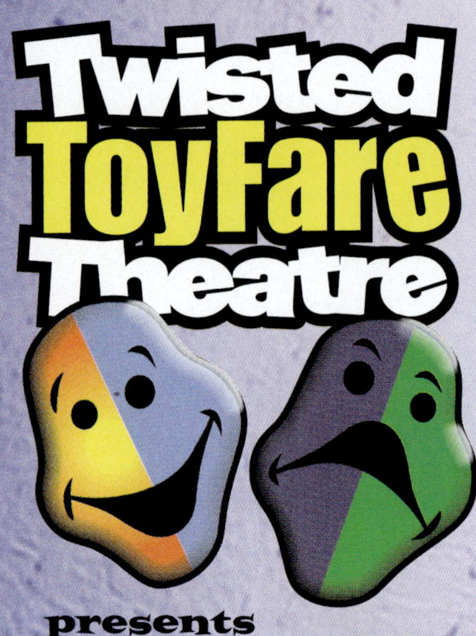

presents

BY: McCALLUM, ROOT & GOLDSTEIN

OKAY, I'LL *URP* BE HERE WHEN YOU--HEY, FIDDLER CRABSH!
HI, LI'L GUYSH, WHAT'SH... WAIT, WHAT ARE YOU...NO... *OH, NO...*

YEEAARRGGHH!!!
SNIP!
SNIP!
SNIP!
SNIP!

AT THAT MOMENT, AT THE OTHER END OF THE BEACH, THE LONG-TERM PLANS OF THE NEFARIOUS SANDMAN FINALLY COME TO FRUITION...
LA LA LA LA...DEE DEE DEE DEE...
THAT'S RIGHT, KID...YEAH, WORK THE PARAPET...

HULK SMASH! HEE HEE HEE!
AHHH! NO!
YAAAGGH!!!
KICK!

THAT *DOES* IT!
I'M SICK OF BEING A 98-POUND WEAKLING!
RHARGHHH, HULK: 27, SAND CASTLES: 0.
M-M-MY... M-M-MY...

SMASH! 28-0!
DUDE, THERE WAS A PUPPY IN THERE.
AND BY YMIR'S BLOOD, HE HATH GOTTEN *SAND* IN THE ODINSON'S *FRESCA!*

HAH-HO!
HULK SMASH THAT ONE NEXT, THEN THAT ONE, THEN--

...THEN...

DAISY SMASH!
COO, COO, COO!
SOMEBODY'S GOT TO PUT A STOP TO YOU DUKES!

DAISY: 31, SAND CASTLES...EH?

BOOOIIIINNGGG!!!

SUMMER LOVIN', HAD ME A BLAST...

...SUMMER LOVIN', HAPPENED SO FAST...

...MET A GIRL, CRAZY FOR ME...
YOU HAD ME AT HELLO...YOU HAD ME AT HELLO...
UMM... WHY THE F ARE WE IN THIS PANEL?
YOU SAID 'F.'
SHOW HULK DA MONEY!

...FORGOT THAT SHARKS LIVE IN THE SEA...

CHOMP!

PLOP!

SNIP!
SNIP!
SNIP!
SNIP!

SUDDENLY...
ATLANTIS ATTACKS!
HOLD IT!!!

NOBODY'S GONNA KICK SAND IN MY FACE AGAIN! THANK YOU, CHARLES ATLAS!
THANK YOU, INDEED! YUM!

PERISH, LAND-WALKER!
LORD, NO!
GUURRK!
SPLURK!

YOURS...IS... SUPERIOR...
SOB S-SUMMER D-D-DAYS, SNIFF DRIFTIN' AWAY...

OH WELLA, WELLA, WELLA...
EH?

TELL ME MORE, TELL ME MORE...
HULK WANT KNOW IF YOU GOT VERY FAR?
UHH...DIDN'T THE LOVE OF YOUR LIFE JUST GET EATEN BY A SHARK? AND YOU'RE DANCING?
SOMEBODY GET ME SOME FIDDLER CRABS.
THE END

BUCKY

Height: 6.75 inches
Weight: 1.7 oz.
Coffin Preference: Solid Mahogany with Red Velvet lining
First Appearance (Pre-Crisis): "The Big Race," *ToyFare* #18
First Appearance (Post-Crisis): "How Von Doom Stole Christmas," *ToyFare* #6
Died: "The Big Race," *ToyFare* #18
Died: "Beach Blanket Mego," *ToyFare* #24
Died: "Working for the Man," *ToyFare* #31
Died: "War is Hell," *ToyFare* #45
Died: "Project Greenlight," *Wizard* Spider-Man Special
Died: "Snow Day," *ToyFare* #54
Died: "'Til Death Do You Part," *ToyFare* #57
Died: "The Hunt for Red Ork-tober," *ToyFare* #62
Died: "Idol Hands," *ToyFare* #67
Died: "Twenty, Twenty, 24 Hours To Go," *ToyFare* #70
Died: "CHiPs, Ahoy!" *ToyFare* #80
History: The phrase "born to die" comes to mind when we mention Bucky. Probably because we just made that phrase up. Getting lasered in half by Vision (*ToyFare* #31), dipped in hot lava by Red Skull (*ToyFare* #54), mauled by a panther (*ToyFare* #80) and stabbed by a swordfish ("Beach Blanket Mego," *ToyFare* #24) is par for the course on any day that ends in "Y." When not dying and bleeding from every orifice, you can find him egging Dr. Doom's castle ("Halloween at Castle Doom," *ToyFare* #4), convincing Spidey to buy him cigarettes ("Project: Green Light," *Spider-Man Special*) or fishing.
Deadliest Weapon: Was, by some cruel twist of fate, the lone survivor of the great "Victor Von Doom Christmas Sled Crash of '97" (*ToyFare* #6). To this day, scientists are baffled.

TOYFARE #54 "Snow Day"

TOYFARE #80 "Chips Ahoy!"

Seder-Masochism

As originally published in *ToyFare* #94

"Former Executive Editor Andrew Kardon, owner of the original Megos used in 'TTT,' pitched a Passover strip, and once we decided to build it around the Thing it practically wrote itself. I was concerned it would be viewed as anti-Semitic instead of self-deprecating because, even though I'm Jewish, I don't have a very Jewish last name, but it actually got passed around the Internet and posted on a lot of Jewish websites. One of my proudest moments. But for the record, Seder food is awesome."

- Justin Aclin

Twisted ToyFare Theatre

PRESENTS

SEDER-MASOCHISM

BY: McCALLUM, OAT & ACLIN

WITH: GUTIERREZ, KARDON & WARD

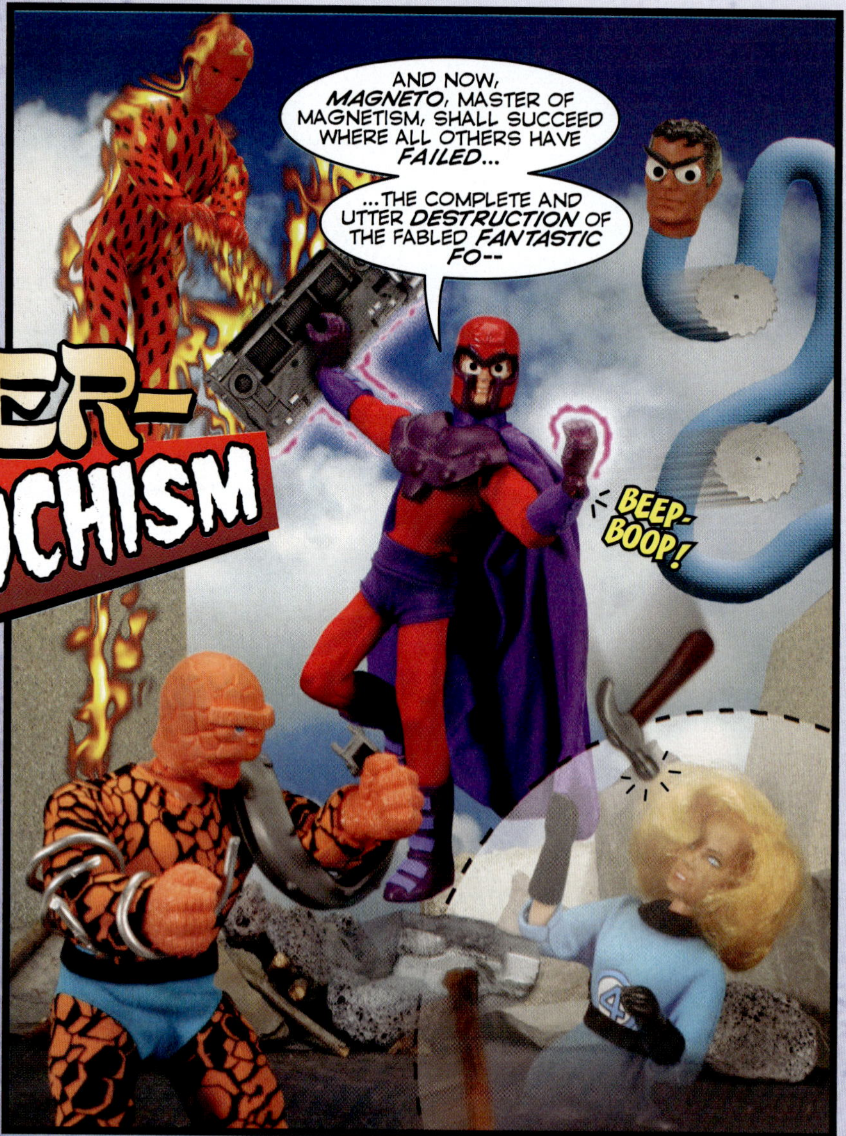

AND NOW, *MAGNETO*, MASTER OF MAGNETISM, SHALL SUCCEED WHERE ALL OTHERS HAVE *FAILED*...

...THE COMPLETE AND UTTER *DESTRUCTION* OF THE FABLED *FANTASTIC* FO--

BEEP-BOOP!

WELL, WE MIGHT AS WELL CLEAN UP ALL THIS RUBBLE.
...
SORRY, STRETCHO, BUT AS A JEW, I CAN'T DO STUFF AT NIGHT.
MY SUPERIOR INTELLECT DETECTS BULL████.
I'M CALLING YOUR PARENTS.

...HELLO?
I CAN'T GET A DIAL TONE.
I DON'T REMEMBER YOU EVER BUILDING A PHONE INTO H.E.R.B.I.E.
TAP
TAP
TAP
DON'T STOP...

AND SO...
OF COURSE OUR BENJY IS JEWISH.
AND VOULD IT KILL YOU TO CALL YOUR PARENTS ONCE IN A WHILE, HANH?
HOLY CRAP, I WAS JUS' MAKIN' THAT UP TA GET OUTTA WOIK!

DAT DOES S'PLAIN A COUPLE TINGS, DOH.
AND HERE I THOUGHT DAT WAS A SIDE-EFFECT'A DA COSMIC RADIATION.

LATER...
WHILE WE'RE AT CHURCH, CAN YOU WATCH FRANKLIN?
HE CAN'T COME BECAUSE HE'S A BASTARD.
HE WAS BORN OUTTA WEDLOCK?
NO, HE'S JUST A BASTARD.

...HELLO?

LATER...
HOW'M I SPOSED TA LEARN TA BE JEWISH?
ALL DEEZ BOOKS ARE WRITTEN IN KREE OR SUMTIN'!
SHALOM!

SWEET MAGILLA GORILLA, THA' NEGATIVE ZONE PORTAL MUST BE LEAKIN' AGAIN!
I'M NO MONSTER, I'M THE SPIRIT OF JUDAISM!

AND IF YOU REALLY WANT TO KNOW WHAT IT'S LIKE TO BE JEWISH, YOU SHOULD THROW A PASSOVER SEDER!
IT'S JUST LIKE THANKSGIVING, BUT WITHOUT THE GOOD FOOD.
WE COULD HAVE IT TONIGHT!

WHY NOT, I GOT NUTHIN' BETTER TA' DO.
LET'S JUST SEE WHICH A' DESE FLARE GUNS... AH-HA!
F.F. FLARE
STAR OF DAVID
GOLDEN ARCHE

DIS OUGHTTA BRING EVERY JEWISH SUPERHERO IN TOWN.
AN' A COUPLE'A MOVIE PRODUCAS.
FOOMF!
FIRE IN THE HOLE!

HIGH ABOVE...
DAMN FARE HIKES...TWO BUCKS TO RIDE THE SUBWAY?!
FORGET IT. I'LL FLY TO THE DELI!
WHY, THE NERVE OF-- EH?

YOU AGAIN?

HEY...DON'T YOU NEED YER FANCY HELMET SO YOUSE DON'T GET *MIND-CONTROLLED* OR SUMTHIN'?

ON *RELIGIOUS* OCCASIONS I ALWAYS WEAR THIS PSYCHIC-PROOF *YARMULKE** INSTEAD.

*PRONOUNCED "YARMULKE."

CAPTAIN'S LOG--JEWISH CALENDAR DATE 5765.

THE AWAY TEAM IS BEAMING DOWN FOR A *PASSOVER* CELE--

VMMMMMMMMM...

YO, DAVID DUKE, YOU JOININ' THE PARTY OR *WHAT?*
WHA...HOW DID YOU *SPOT* ME HERE IN THE *SHADOWS?!*
NEWSFLASH, MARGARET: YER' WEARIN' *WHITE*.

WHITE I MAY BE, BUT *NO ONE* MUST SUSPECT THE TRUTH...THAT JEWISH MILLIONAIRE MARC SPECTOR IS REALLY THE CLOAKED VIGILANTE *MOON KNIGHT!*
LIKE ANYONE GIVES A CRAP.
NOW GIT DOWNSTAIRS BEFORE THE BATMAN LAWYERS SPOT YA'.

WELCOME *ALLA YOUSE* TO MY-- WHO DA HELL IS DIS BROAD?
I'M *SABRA*, ISRAELI SUPER SOLDIER AND GUARDIAN OF THE HOLY LAND!

I BROUGHT WINE.
GREAT!

OKAY BEN, THE FIRST THING TO DO ON PASSOVER IS POUR A GLASS OF WINE FOR THE PROPHET *ELIJAH!*
LEGEND HAS IT HE GOES DOOR TO DOOR AND--

WHAM!
I'M HERE F'R THE *HIC* *BOOZE*.
LESH GET THISH OVER WITH...I'VE GOT SIXTY MORE SEDERS ON THISH BLOCK *ALONE*.

GLUG
GLUG
GLUG

THUD

YOU OKAY, LITTLE HOBBIT GUY?
AND HEY, GOOD JOB ON KILLIN' MACAULAY CULKIN IN DAT MOVIE.

...MUH...MUH...

WOW... HE'S REALLY DRUNK.
RIGHT YOU ARE, KITTY PRYDE!
NOW'S THE TIME TO READ THE STORY OF THE JEWS' EXODUS FROM EGYPT!

IF IT MEANS SAVING PASSOVER, I'LL DO IT.
HOLD THIS, NIMOY.
...WHY DON'T YOU HOLD THIS?

FORTY MINUTES LATER...
...SO MOSES ASKED THE PHARAOH A FORTIETH TIME TO FREE HIS PEOPLE, BUT STILL BLAH, BLAH, BLAH...
FER THE LUVA MIKE, I'M STARVIN' TA DEATH OVA' HERE WAITIN' FOR DIS PHARAOH GUY!
'SCUSE ME A SEC'...

AT THAT MOMENT, 3,000 YEARS AGO...
...PLEASE?
NO.
PLEASE?
NO!

YO, YOU RAMA-TUT?
HANG ON, LEMME CHECK MY SCHEDULE...
VMMMMMM

HMMM...
DECEMBER
KANG
RAMA-TUT
STEVE MARTIN
IRON LAD

YEP, I'M RA--
DAT'S FER THA' 'SCORPION KING.'
SOCK!
OH, AND LET MY PEOPLE GO, YA MOOK!

MOMENTS LATER, IN THE PRESENT...
...BUT THEN THE ORANGE ONE APPEARED, THE JEWS WERE ALLOWED TO LEAVE EGYPT AND EVERYONE LIVED HAPPILY EVER AFTER.
UH... THE END.
YAY, NOW LET'S--

NOT SO FAST!
THE ALL-SEEING EYE OF AGAMOTTO SENSES AN OTHERWORLDLY PRESENCE!
SLAM!

YOU CAN'T HIDE FROM ME, SPIRIT!
SAESEE TIIN!
URK...!
ZZZAP!

AWWW, HE... HE WASN'T AN EVIL DEMON, HE WAS JUST SOME CUTE LITTLE PIXIE.
NOW I FEEL KIND OF *GUILTY*...
THEN THE SPIRIT OF JUDAISM LIVES ON!

EPILOGUE...
WE'RE BACK FROM CHURCH.
OH YEAH, I FERGOT ABOUT DAT PLOT POINT.
HEADS UP, TORCHY...ELIJAH WOOD PASSED OUT IN YER ROOM.
GREAT.

THERE BETTER NOT BE ANY FRESH PUKE ON THOSE PILLOWS.
HEY, I KNOW YOU HEARD ME, RADIO FLYER, I *SEE* YOU'RE AWAKE.
I SAID...
...WHA...?

I SEE YOU!

...I GOTTA LAY OFF THE SAUCE.
END

MR. SPOCK

Height: 7.75 inches
Weight: 2.1 oz.
Known Associates: James T. Kirk, Leonard "Bones" McCoy, Sasquatch, Bilbo Baggins
Expert In: Vulcan nerve pinch, early childhood development
First Appearance: "The Big Race," *ToyFare* #18
Died: "Blinded by Science," *ToyFare* #17
Died: "Viva Mego!" *ToyFare* #33
Died: "I Am Legend, Part One," *ToyFare* #84
History: The Jan Brady of the Mego Universe, you might think that Mr. Spock has suffered his entire career in the shadow of the more charismatic, more flamboyant and more frequently nude Captain Kirk. But you'd be wrong! Spock had a brief run as a solo character before he ever hooked up with Kirk in these pages. Spock first appeared in *ToyFare* #17, when Reed Richards' faulty mathematics convinced him that the citizens of Megoville were actually toys, which caused Mr. Spock to remove his pants and renounce logic. He was subsequently hit by a car. He next appeared in *ToyFare* #18, dressed up like Namor the Sub-Mariner since *ToyFare* was too cheap to shell out for an actual custom. Then, in *ToyFare* #19, Spock was finally united with the *Enterprise* Bridge Crew, identifying a space-bound Doctor Doom as a satellite designed to yell profanity. Since then, Spock has often appeared in the company of Captain Kirk, desperately waiting for the time when it will be more logical to kill him than to let him live.
Claim to Fame: "Got together" with Kirstie Alley, back when that meant something.

TOYFARE #17 "Blinded By Science"

TOYFARE #59 "Trek or Treat"

A Few Good Megos

As originally published in *ToyFare* #43

"What with all our custom jobs, we had the best Mego collection in the known universe, and it was a lot of fun to mobilize a huge cast once in a while. Our primary goal was always to be funny, but our reward for being funny was getting to write a superhero comic book month after month."

- Tom Root

"Monkeys are always funny."

- Doug Goldstein

A FEW GOOD MEGOS

BY PAT McCALLUM, TOM ROOT & DOUGLAS GOLDSTEIN

Photos by Paul Schiraldi.

AND SO THE CALL GOES OUT...
THE FABLED FANTASTIC FOUR!
THE MIGHTY AVENGERS!
THE UNCANNY X-MEN!
THE DEFENDERS!

SHORTLY...
WE'LL HELP IN ANY WAY WE CAN, OFFICER!
THANKS, MUTIE. SAY... ARE WE MISSING SOMEBODY?

DEEP IN THE SUBURBS...
UMMM... TRY A LEFT AT THE DAIRY MART.
HULK HAVE TO PEE AGAIN.
WHAT?!? THAT'S THE SAME DAIRY MART WE PASSED TWENTY MINUTES AGO!

IF WE COMBINE OUR FORCES, WE CAN--
YEAH, YEAH, SURE.
LEAVE THIS TO THE BIG BOYS, BALDY!

AND THAT WOULD BE THE FANTASTIC FOUR!
WATCH IT! I'LL LAY YOU OUT LIKE A THAI SCHOOL-GIRL!
SHOVE!

HAW HAW! I DO IT 'CAUSE IT MAKES ME LAUGH!
PLOP!
WHUFF!

HOLY $@#%!!
GOOD THING MY PEE TURNS TO STEAM WHEN I FLAME ON!
FASTBALL SPECIAL, BUB!
WAS IT MY IMAGINATION OR DID COLOSSUS COP A FEEL?
GODSPEED, TRUSTY SHIELD!
WAIT!! I'M ON YOUR TEAMAAARGH!
ZARRRK!
WHIZZZZZ!
SO, WANDA...DOES YOUR FRIEND WANT TO COME OVER FOR DRINKS?
HAW! SOMEONE'S BEEN A BAD GIRL!
SPANK!
SPANK!
SPANK!
AHH! AHH! AHH! ...OOH!
SAY IT, OR I'LL BEAT YOU BLACKER THAN YOUR ROOTS!
...KISS ME.

RIP HER TOP OFF, WANDA! HER TOP!
SEEK AND DES--*URP*-- DES--*URP*-- STROY!
BAMF!
Lay's
AIM FOR HIS SOFT MIDDLE, TOVARISCH!
WAIT, WAIT! WE SHOULD ALL WORK TOGETH-- UNGH!
CLANG!
GOOD THING YOU'RE 'HANDI-ABLED'-- OR I'D FEEL GUILTY ABOUT THIS!
K-POW! K-POW!
IDIOT! YOUR FISTS ARE MADE OF RUBBER!

AW YEAH! TWENTY BUCKS ON THE REDHEAD!
QUIET OUT HERE OR I'LL GET THE HOSE!
HEY! YOU'RE UNDER ARREST!

LATER...
ORDER! ORDER, DAMMIT, OR I'LL CLEAR THIS ENTIRE COURTROOM!
BANG!
BANG!
BANG!

UHHH... NOBODY WAS SAYING ANYTHING.

SSSTRING HIM UP!
SPIDER-MAN IS A MENACE!
KILL HIM!
STOP IT.
WAS THAT YOUR LEG? SORRY.

PSST... I'M REALLY DAREDEVIL!
...GREAT.

YOUR HONOR, WE CALL AS OUR FIRST WITNESS... SPIDER-MAN!

NOW, SPIDER-MAN, WHERE WERE YOU THE EVENING OF THE TWELFTH?
WITH YOUR MOM AT THE HYATT?

WHY, YOU...! LADIES AND GENTLEMEN, I PRESENT TO YOU... EXHIBIT 'A'!

THIS SECURITY FOOTAGE CLEARLY DEPICTS SPIDER-MAN COMMITTING A CRIME MOST FOUL!
ATM

WAITAMINNIT... HOW AM I SUPPOSED TO BE TWO SPIDER-MEN?

HOW INDEED?
OH FOR...! HEY, ARE YOU A REGULAR MONKEY OR THE BIG-ASSED KIND?

WHY, I OUGHTA--
STOP THE TRIAL!
NOW WHAT?

I JUST CAUGHT THESE TWO JOHN TRAVOLTAS ROBBING A CONVENIENCE STORE!
UP YER NOSE...
...WID A RUBBA HOSE!

TWO TRAVOLTAS? TWO SPIDER-MEN? THIS CAN ONLY MEAN ONE THING...

SKRULLS!
LUCKILY, MY INTELLECT--WHICH IS FAR ABOVE THAT OF DR. DOOM--WAS AT THE READY!
IN YER EAR...
...WID A CAN A BEER!

QUIET! LET SCIENCE HANDLE THIS!
MY GUN!
IN YER-- AGH!
WID A-- UGH!
BLAM! BLAM!

UMM...
ERR...
UH-OH.

HEY... HOW COME THAT ONE'S NOT CHANGING BACK?
UM, LET'S BURY THE BODIES *QUICKLY*, SHALL WE?

THE SKRULLS WERE THE BANK ROBBERS AND SPIDER-MAN IS *INNOCENT!* CASE DISMI--

BLAM!

BLAM!
BLAM!
BLAM!
BLAM!
A COURTROOM WHERE *APES* EVOLVED FROM *MEN?* NOT ON *MY* WATCH!
CHUCK HESTON AND THE *N.R.A.!*

THAT'S RIGHT, *RUN*, YOU HAIRY BASTARDS, *RUN!*
BLAM!
BLAM!
WAIT, I HAVE A FAM-- *ACK!*
SAVE ME, MONKEY JES-- *URK!*

THE *N.R.A....* WORKING FOR A *MONKEYLESS FUTURE!*
END

PONCH AND JON

Height: 8 inches (Ponch); 8 inches (Jon)
Weight: 2.5 oz. (Ponch); 2.4 oz. (Jon)
Group Affiliation: The California Highway Patrol (or CHiPs, #3 in the most awkward acronyms of all time)
Licensed To: Perform nostalgic cameos, beat '80s toys with nightsticks
First Appearance: "Super Villain Jeopardy," *ToyFare* #1
Died: "Viva Mego!" *ToyFare* #33
Died: "I Am Legend, Part One," *ToyFare* #84
History: Quick, who appeared first in "Twisted ToyFare"—the Hulk or Ponch and Jon? If you said the Hulk, that's a very reasonable assumption. But it's wrong! Megoville's most prominent law enforcement officers (despite the fact that Megoville is in New York and they work for the California Highway Patrol) showed up in the very first full-length "TTT" ("Super Villain Jeopardy," *ToyFare* #1)! Since then, whenever the long arm of the law is needed to rein in one of Megoville's most wanted, you can count on Ponch and Jon showing up. Or occasionally just Ponch. Because, really, Jon is kind of boring.

The CHiPs boys once found their monopoly on police work in the city in jeopardy when they gunned down an innocent penguin who was trying to give them an ice cream cone (*ToyFare* #22). They were replaced by Mexican Luchadores El Hombre Spectacular Incredible and his partner Gary. However, after besting the duo in a wrestling match, Ponch and Jon unmasked them and revealed them to be Starsky and Hutch. They then gunned them down.
Names Short for: Arthur Poncharelli and Jonathan, respectively

TOYFARE #56 "Shanks For The Memories"

TOYFARE #80 "Chips Ahoy!"

MR. SPIDEY GOES TO CORUSCANT

As originally published in *ToyFare* #26

"You had to comment on *Episode One*. It was a shock to Star Wars fans because there was basically the assumption that a new Star Wars film would be revolutionary and return the joys of everything, and everything would be like it was when we were kids. And it just didn't do that. A lot of things in the movie were ridiculous, and Spider-Man is the everyman who goes there and points this all out."

- Doug Goldstein

Twisted ToyFare Theatre

THE GALACTIC SENATE WILL NOW COME TO ORDER!

WE RECOGNIZE THE DELEGATE FROM THE SOVEREIGN SYSTEM OF NABOO.

MR. SPIDEY GOES TO CORUSCANT

by Pat McCallum, Tom Root and Douglas Goldstein

All photos by Paul Schiraldi. Lucas photo courtesy of the Everett Collection.

THE SENATE DOES ***NOT*** RECOGNIZE THE DELEGATES FROM MEGOVILLE!
YEAH, WHATEVER.
LOOK, THIS MOVIE ***BLOWS***. FOR THE NEXT ONE SCRAP SOME OF THE CGI MUPPETS AND USE THE EXTRA CASH FOR A BETTER SCRIPT.
BUT KEEP THAT JAKE LLOYD PUPPET. THAT THING LOOKSH-- ***JUMPIN' CATFISH!***

THAT'SH NO MOON! I MEAN... ***THAT'SH NO CHANCELLOR--THAT'SH GENERAL ZOD!***

THERE'SH NOWHERE TO *HIC* ***RUN, ZOD!***
WAIT, IRON MAN, HE'S NOT--UH, NEVER MIND. GO GET 'IM, CHAMP.

DON'T PRETEND LIKE THISH *HIC* GRIP IS CRACKING YOUR BONES, ZOD! I KNOW YOU'RE INVULNERABLE!
KRAK
ARGH!
AND ***YOU!*** DO YOU REALLY THINK THE MOVIEGOERS DON'T KNOW YOU'RE DARTH SIDIOUS?
WHAT?!?

I-- YOU--I AM ***NOT***-- I MEAN--***DARTH MAUL, GET HIM!***

TINK

YOU'D THINK HE'D DO MORE THAN JUST STAND THERE, HUH?

YO CHINEE FOOD, MISSA SPIDAH-MAN!*
WONTON SOUP EES PAH-FECTLY REGAL.*
*HEY, DON'T BLAME US. THAT'S WHAT THEY SOUND LIKE.

CRUNCH! MUNCH! CRUNCH!
THE GALACTIC SENATE ***WILL NOT*** STAND FOR THESE INTRUSIONS!

CRUNCH! CHOMP! MUNCH!
MUNCH!
AND FURTHERMORE... *AHEM*...AND FURTHERMORE, WE WILL NOT--
CRUNCH!

MUNCH! CHOMP!
CRUNCH!
MUNCH!
WHAT THE HELL IS THAT NOISE?!?
CRUNCH!
CRUNCH!
MUNCH!
CHOMP!
CRUNCH!
MUNCH! SQUISH! CHOMP!
CRUNCH!
MUNCH! CRUNCH!
MUNCH!
CHOMP!
CRUNCH!

GOOD LORD!
RHARGHH RAK NA RHARGHH MAKKI-MAKKI!*
ELLIOTTTT...
RHAKI-BAKI!**
MUNCH!
CRUNCH!
MUNCH!
CRUNCH!
MUNCH!
*"WOOKIES BET E.T. SENATORS SUPPORT TERM LIMITS NOW! HOO-HA!"
**"THE SECRET OF THE FLYING BICYCLE DIES WITH YOU!"

YOU AND YOUR FRIENDS ON THE FOREST MOON OF ENDOR WILL PAY DEARLY FOR THIS TRANSGRESSION!
LOOK, ALL I'M SAYING IS THE ORIGINAL 'STAR WARS' CAPTURED THE YOUTH MARKET WITH-OUT CATERING ONLY TO CHIL--

VMMMMM

MMMMMM

IF YOU WILL NOT BE TURNED, YOU WILL BE--
...DESTROYED. YEAH, YEAH, I KNOW.
HEY...HOW COME THE JEDI COUNCIL CAN'T SENSE YOU IF YOU'RE SO POWERFUL?
AND WHY DIDN'T QUI-GON DISAPPEAR WHEN HE DIED? AND WHY--
ENOUGH!!

*"WHAT EVERYONE SHOULD REMEMBER IS THAT "EPISODE I" WAS PRIMARILY INTENDED FOR YOUNGER VIEWERS AND ISN'T INTENDED TO BE A SELF-CONTAINED MOVIE, BUT A SPRINGBOARD FOR TWO MORE FILMS THAT FLESH OUT THE GROUND-WORK LAID IN THIS ONE. JUST RELAX, HAVE AN OPEN MIND AND IF YOU STOP PICKING IT APART FOR JUST A SECOND, YOU MIGHT ACTUALLY ENJOY IT."

SUDDENLY...
DOO-DOO-DOO-DOOOOOOOOO!

AAAA-EEEE-AAHH!
IK WAK CHEW NACCA!
I GOT A WING!

YUB YUB!
HEY, YOU'RE RIGHT! THANKS TO JAR JAR, EWOKS AREN'T THE SUCKIEST PART OF THE STAR WARS UNIVERSE ANYMORE. CONGRATS.
THAT AND WE KNOW THINGS CAN'T GET ANY WORSE.

THINK SO? JUST WAIT UNTIL 'EPISODE II'! HAW HAW!

EPILOGUE: MAY 16TH, 2002. OPENING NIGHT FOR "STAR WARS EPISODE II: THE PEEPS OF WRATH."
THE FORCE IS STRONG IN THESE DELICIOUS MARSHMALLOW JEDI!
THE WORST PART IS THAT IN THE FUTURE MOVIE TICKETS COST $40 APIECE.
THE ODINSON KNEW WE SHOULD HAVE SEEN 'TITANIC II' INSTEAD!
THE END

EWOKS

History: To those born after 1983, the Ewok tribe represents a noble race of underdogs who led the Rebels to freedom via rock slingshots and made kids everywhere chuckle in delight. To those born *before* 1983, Ewoks are the equivalent of a Jim Henson eye-rape, and fanboys would take part in a whine-fest about Lucas and his penchant for Teddy Bears that would not end until the introduction of Jar Jar Binks.

Appearances: The Ewok tribe usually appears when a script calls for something to be roped to a spit, rotisseried over an open flame and savagely eaten. That, or if a good ol' fashioned "Yub Yub" needs to occur. This would first take place in *ToyFare* #26 ("Mr. Spidey Goes to Coruscant") when Jar Jar is devoured, Binks and all. In "DVD-Day" (*ToyFare* #58), the dirty bears eat a Stormtrooper alive—but Wilford Brimley plays the karma card by stuffing and eating an Ewok in *ToyFare* #96 ("Running With Xixors"). When Hulk smashes Chief Chirpa in *ToyFare* #48 ("Craptus Interuptus"), they roast the green-skinned goliath on Endor.

TOYFARE #26 "Mr. Spidey Goes to Coruscant"

WICKET
The cool and unofficial leader—like the Zack Morris of Ewoks. He also had kind of a thing for Princess Leia's helmet, revealing his weird hat fetish to the world.

CHIEF CHIRPA (deceased)
"Although bylaws allow him to partake of our women at any time he chooses, he rarely did," recalls Wicket of Chirpa's character.

PAPLOO
Is all bear, but has creepy, human-like lips. We'd rather not know why that is, or why Nein Numb was found alone with his mother.

LOGRAY
The tribe's chief doctor, his actions are firmly rooted in the logic of science and medicine...except when he's worshipping a floating, gay robot.

TEEBO
Looks cute, but secretly kept a Stormtrooper in his hut as "entertainment" for three years until the Trooper managed to take his own life.

STINKY
Not just a clever nickname—he absolutely smells like wet dogs--t.

Get Smart!

As originally published in *ToyFare* #108

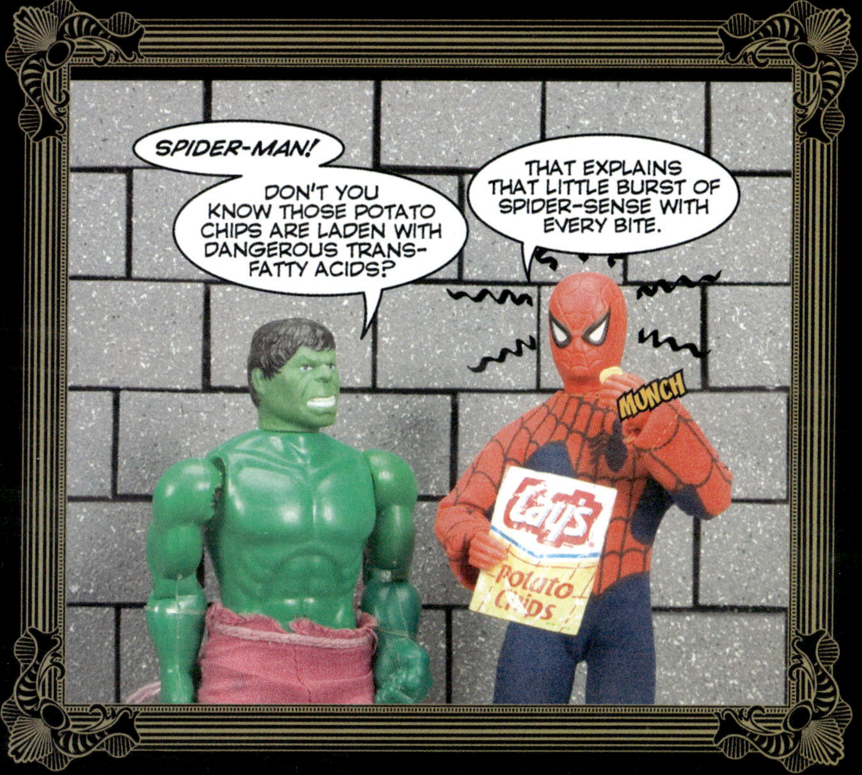

"Sometimes, you need to cross a line for good comedy, and we crossed several lines in this strip. But each time the jokes had us rolling on the floor laughing, so it's okay, right? Right? *Sigh*...we're horrible people. At least we got to re-use our favorite 'TTT' ending ever—'Employee of the Month!' The original version appears in an early 'TTT' strip, 'The Super Friends,' that will most likely never be reprinted, so this was our way to keep it alive."

- Zach Oat

BY: McCALLUM, OAT & ACLIN

WITH: GUTIERREZ, KARDON, & WARD

SPECIAL THANKS TO: ARBONA, BRICKEN, COLLINS, PENAGOS, PURDIN & TRACEY

...AND SO, SINCE TOMATOES ARE, UNBEKNOWNST TO MOST, A FRUIT, I--WHOM MEN CALL *THE LEADER*--COUNT THEM AS *ONE* ITEM ALONGSIDE MY BANANAS, THUS KEEPING ME *UNDER* THE 'TWELVE ITEMS OR LESS' MANDATE SET BY THIS ESTABLISHMENT'S CHECK-OUT LINE.

12 ITEMS OR LESS

HEY, TAKE IT *EASY* ON HIM!
YOU KNOW HE CAN'T HELP THE WAY HE IS.
AND *I* CAN'T HELP TELLING YOU TO SHOVE IT.
SO *SHOVE IT*, MADAM, SHOVE *EVERY* PART OF IT!

I'M *PERFECTLY* CAPABLE OF CARRYING MY OWN BAGS, YOU *SLACKWIT!*
GROCERY STOR
RHARGHH, HULK PRIDE HIMSELF ON *EXCELLENCE* OF SERVICE!
HULK EVEN USE PAPER *AND* PLASTIC TO KEEP EGG DRIPPINGS IN BAG!

SIGH
JUST PUT THE VISCOUS REMAINS IN MY--
WHRRR
24 HR TO
MY *PRIUS...!*

PERHAPS YOU FAILED TO NOTICE THE *'POLICEMAN'S BENEVOLENT ASSOCIATION'* STICKER ON MY BUMPER...?
TRY NOT PARKING IN A HANDICAPPED ZONE NEXT TIME.
AND ME AND THE BOYS ARE KEEPING THE *BON JOVI* CD ON YOUR DASH...THAT'S POLICY.

BUT... BUT THE HULK'S PARKED ACROSS *THREE* HANDICAPPED SPOTS!
AND THREE HANDICAPPED *PEOPLE!*
DEFENDERS
TO ME, MY X--
HEY, A *QUARTER...!*

GIVE THE GUY A BREAK, HE'S *SLOW*.
WHAT'S *YOUR* EXCUSE?
WELL, MY *SUPERIOR INTELLECT* PUTS ME ABOVE THE LAWS OF SIMPLE *PLEBEIANS* SUCH AS...
VRRM
24 HR TOWING
OH, I SEE, THE QUESTION WAS *RHETORICAL*.

RHARGHH!
HULK PUT GROCERIES IN TRUNK OF YOUR CAR, IMPOSSIBLE MAN!
BUT...HOW CAN THAT BE?
...UNLESS MY VEHICLE IS SIMULTANEOUSLY BEING TOWED AWAY AND NOT BEING TOWED AWAY...LIKE SCHRODINGER'S CAR.
WAIT--DID YOU PUT THEM IN THE WRONG--

HAW!
HEY HULK, T'ANK YER FRUITY FRIEND FER ALL DA FREE GROCERIES!
'FRUITY?!?'
I'LL HAVE YOU KNOW ONLY A REAL MAN WOULD BE SECURE ENOUGH TO WEAR A JUMPSUIT THIS SNUG!

AHEM.

OH, FOR...!

ONE TENSE WAIT AT A BUS STOP LATER...
CURSE THAT HULK...!
HE THWARTS ME AT EVERY TURN BECAUSE PEOPLE PUT UP WITH HIS MISTAKES, SIMPLY BECAUSE HE'S A RAGING 'TARD.

IF ONLY THERE WAS SOME WAY I COULD MAKE HIM ACCOUNTABLE FOR HIS ACTIONS, I'D-- THAT'S IT!
I'LL BUILD... A DE-TARD RAY!

WHY, WITH SUCH A WEAPON I COULD--*CRAP*, THAT WAS MY STOP!
DRIVER, DRIVER...!

LATER...
SO, UH... WHATCHA GOT THERE, HULK?
RHARGHH, HULK TAKE SECOND JOB AS *DOG-WALKER*.
WHEN DO YOU START?
WHAT SPIDEY MEAN? HULK START *THIRTY MILES* AGO.
BUS STOP
Lay's Potato Chips

HEY, HULK... INCREASE YOUR SPEED OF COGITATION!
YOU'LL GET THAT IN ABOUT THIRTY SECONDS!
WUG-WUG-WUG
BWUH...?

HA, *NOW* LET'S SEE PEOPLE CUT YOU ANY *SLACK!*
AND NOW *I'M* OFF TO THE IMPOUND LOT!
RHARGHH, HULK FEEL... HULK FEEL... THAT IS TO SAY, *I* FEEL... DISCOMBOBULATED.

SPIDER-MAN!
DON'T YOU KNOW THOSE POTATO CHIPS ARE LADEN WITH DANGEROUS TRANS-FATTY ACIDS?
THAT EXPLAINS THAT LITTLE BURST OF SPIDER-SENSE WITH EVERY BITE.
MUNCH
Lay's Potato Chips

I SUDDENLY FEEL THE NEED TO STIMULATE MY *INTELLECT*.
CARE TO ACCOMPANY ME TO THE LATEST *LARS VON TRIER* FILM?
I'LL PASS.
EVERY TIME WE HANG OUT IT LEADS TO RAW MEAT AND VEGETABLES IN MY HOT TUB.

WHAT A FOOL I WAS TO THINK I COULD MAKE THE 'WORLD'S LARGEST SOUP'...WHAT DOES THAT EVEN MEAN?
AND WHAT HAPPENED TO THESE DOGS?!?
THERE'S ONLY ONE MAN WITH MENTAL ACUITY ENOUGH TO UNDERSTAND MY PLIGHT AND OFFER SUCCOR...THE GOLDEN-AGE FLASH!

SHORTLY, AT THE PSYCHIATRIC PRACTICE OF LEONARD "DOC" SAMSON...
SOOO... YOU'RE NOT THE GOLDEN-AGE FLASH?
NO, BUT I GET THAT A LOT.
...IFICATE OF DIPLOMA
TO BE HONEST, IT'S PROBABLY MY OWN FAULT.

BUT LISTEN, HULK... TO GET OVER THE GUILT YOU FEEL, YOU NEED TO MAKE AMENDS TO ALL THOSE YOU'VE WRONGED.
YOU MEAN LIKE ON 'MY NAME IS EARL'?
SIGH
YES, LIKE ON 'MY NAME IS EARL.'

WHY, IT'S A SOLUTION SO SIMPLE, IT'S BRILLIANT!
BUT WHERE TO BEGIN...?
WELL, YOU COULD START BY PAYING THE $200 BILL FOR THIS SESSION AND--

THANKS AGAIN, DOC!
I DON'T KNOW HOW I CAN EVER REPAY YOU!
WHY DON'T YOU LITERALLY REPAY M--
SO LONG!

LATER, AT THE MILITARY BASE OF GENERAL THADDEUS "THUNDERBOLT" ROSS...
UMMM... ARE YOU SURE YOU WANT TO COME IN HERE?
YOU KNOW THE ARMY'S HUNTING YOU, RIGHT?
SIR, WITH THEIR LOWERED RECRUITMENT STANDARDS AND HIGH DIVORCE RATES, THE ARMY IS HARDLY MY MATCH.
PLUS I CAN KICK A TANK TO MICHIGAN.
SO PLEASE, OPEN THE GATE LEST I SMASH YOU.

AND SO...
YOU MAY AS WELL SURRENDER, HULK...YOU DON'T STAND A CHANCE!
YES, BUT HAVE YOU EVER CONSIDERED THE REASON YOU HATE ME SO IS THAT WHILE YOU NEED AN ARMY TO FEEL POWERFUL, I AM MY OWN ARMY?
IN ESSENCE, GENERAL, I REPRESENT EVERYTHING YOU STRIVE TO BE, BUT ULTIMATELY, CANNOT.

MY GOD...!
IT'S ALL TRUE... MY LIFE IS A WASTE!
ALSO...YOU KNOW YOU'RE GAY, RIGHT?
THAT EXPLAINS THIS MUSTACHE...!

C'MERE, TALBOT!
!
SMOO-OOO-OOCH!

I DON'T KNOW HOW I CAN EVER THANK YOU FOR FREEING ME, HULK.
WANNA COME OUT AND HIT THE CLUBS WITH US?
YEAH, I DON'T... I DON'T SMASH THAT WAY.

SUDDENLY...
CRASH!
GASP... IT'S EMIL BLONSKY, THE ABOMINATION!
ANY LAST WORDS, COMRADE?
ACTUALLY...

THREE HOURS LATER...
<...AND SO YOU SEE, COMMUNISM WORKS ON PAPER ONLY, EMIL, BUT IMPERFECT LEADERS CAUSE IT TO FAIL. IT'S THE MUTUAL SELF-INTEREST OF CAPITALISTS THAT FUELS AMERICA'S STRENGTH.>*
<MARX, YOU WERE SO SHORT-SIGHTED...!>
*TRANSLATED FROM THE RUSSIAN.

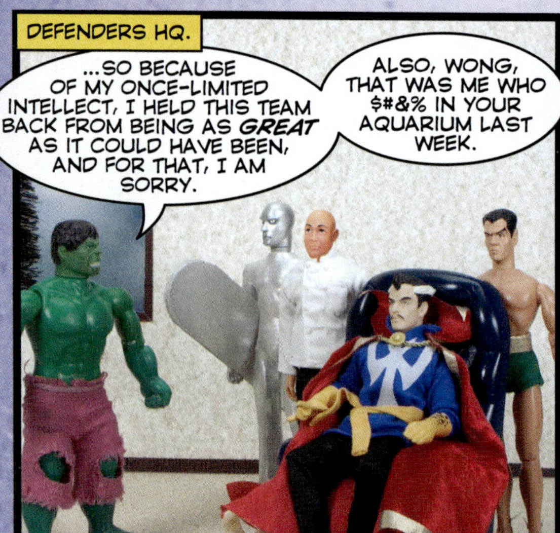
DEFENDERS HQ.
...SO BECAUSE OF MY ONCE-LIMITED INTELLECT, I HELD THIS TEAM BACK FROM BEING AS GREAT AS IT COULD HAVE BEEN, AND FOR THAT, I AM SORRY.
ALSO, WONG, THAT WAS ME WHO $#&% IN YOUR AQUARIUM LAST WEEK.

...
LOOKS LIKE I OWE SOMEBODY AN APOLOGY.
HRMPH

LET'S SEE, WHO'S NEXT ON MY... THE PANTHEON?!?
WHO THE %#@& ARE 'THE PANTHEON'?!?*
GEN. ROSS
ABOMINATION
DEFENDERS
PANTHEON
BETTY
JARELLA
*THEY'RE EITHER A DC TEAM OR SOME GUYS WHO USED TO FIGHT THE SAVAGE DRAGON.

SOON...
MY DEAREST BETTY, THERE IS SOMETHING I'VE ALWAYS WANTED TO ASK YOU, BUT UNTIL NOW NEVER HAD THE WORDS...
OH HULK, ANYTHING, ANYTHING...!

SHORTLY...
I...I STILL DON'T KNOW HOW I AGREED TO THIS...
WELL, I AM VERY SMART.

AND WHO'S YOUR FRIEND AGAIN...?
THAT'S BI-BEAST. HE'S COOL.
RELAX, WHITE SUGAR, IT'S ALL GOOD.

ELSEWHERE...
AND NOW BACK TO THE GAMMY AWARDS, HONORING THE FINEST ACHIEVEMENTS OF GAMMA-IRRADIATED AMERICANS!
HMMM... IT APPEARS MY INVITATION WAS LOST IN THE MAIL.
AGAIN.
SIP

AND THE AWARD FOR THE SMARTEST GAMMA-IRRADIATED SCIENTIST GOES TO...THE HULK!
SPBBBBB...!
WHAT?!?

I THOUGHT IT WAS BAD WHEN HE CALLED IN BEFORE ME TO IDENTIFY THE Q-103 LUNCH LICK, BUT THIS IS UNACCEPTABLE!
I HAVE NO CHOICE...I MUST RE-RETARD THE HULK!

LATER...
SO YOU SEE, IRON MAN, YOUR DESIRE TO 'BUST' ME USING THIS 'HULKBUSTER ARMOR' IS AN EXAMPLE OF YOUR IRRATIONAL BELIEF THAT YOU CAN CONTROL NATURE THROUGH TECHNOLOGY.
URP
H'OKAY.

HA!
TIME TO GET DUMB COURTESY OF MY NEW RETARDO RAY!
SLAM!
HOLY CRA-URP! IT'SH SHE-HULK!
LET ME HANDLE THIS.

LEADER, I KNOW THE CONTEMPT YOU FEEL, HOW YOUR DIZZYING INTELLECT HAS SET YOU APART FROM THE REST OF HUMANITY...HOW NO ONE COULD POSSIBLY KNOW THE DEPTHS OF YOUR LONELINESS.
NO ONE... BUT ME.

YOU...YOU UNDERSTAND?
OH THANK YOU, HULK, THANK YOU... WITH YOU AS MY FRIEND, I'LL NEVER HAVE TO FEEL SO ALONE AGAIN!
NO, YOU WON'T.

STILL, WE CAN'T HAVE YOU WALKING AROUND WITH SOMETHING SO DANGEROUS, CAN WE?
WHA?
SWIPE!

NEITHER CAN WE HAVE YOU BUILDING ANOTHER ONE, SO...
GAH...!
ZAP!

NO...!
MY GLORIOUS INTELLECT... FADING!
FADING LIKE... THAT THING... LIKE... SOFT... BUNNIES... SO SOFT...

AND SO...
HEY, YOU FIT IT ALL IN ONE BAG...!
NICE JOB, RETARD.
MY NAME IS LEEDER

EMPLOYEE OF THE MONTH
EGGS ON TOP!
MY NAME IS LEEDER
END

The New Neighbors

As originally published in *ToyFare* #14

"Tom Root didn't understand at the time that the Borg designations like Two of Five just meant that there are five Borgs and that's the second. So a few in the strip are like, ' I am Sixteen of Ten,' which obviously makes no sense. If people took it as a joke, fantastic. But later on I pointed out to Tom that it doesn't make sense and he had no idea why it didn't make sense."

- Doug Goldstein

THE NEW NEIGHBORS

By Pat McCallum, Tom Root and Douglas Goldstein

WE ARE BORG. RESISTANCE IS FUTILE. PREPARE TO BE ASSIM--

SLAM!

KNOCK
KNOCK
KNOCK

DON'T DO THAT. WE ARE BORG. RESISTANCE IS FUTILE.

SLA--
PREPARE TO BE ASSIM--

THUD!

WE HAVE ADAPTED TO YOUR OFFENSIVE CAPABILITIES. PREPARE TO BE ASSIMILATED.
THOR! IT'S FOR YOU!

THE NEXT DAY...
LOOKS LIKE THOSE LITTLE ROBOT GUYS ARE HAVING A PARTY.

HOW WOULD YOU LIKE YOUR GROUND BOVINE PATTY, THREE OF TWELVE?
VERILY, MEDIUM-WELL... WITH CHEESE.
NINE OF EIGHT OWES THE COLLECTIVE AN APOLOGY. NINE OF EIGHT HAS LOST THE KICKBALL.
NINE OF EIGHT IS A 'TARD.
KISS THE CHEF
PEPSI

THAT SMELLS GREAT. AND THAT'S A PRETTY COOL BARBECUE.

HEY... WAITAMINNIT!

THAT'S *MY* BARBECUE!

LIKE I REALLY NEEDED A REASON TO HATE 'STAR TREK.' I--*EH?*

HEY... THAT'S MY CAR!!!
FOUR OF FIVE CANNOT GET A GOOD ROCK STATION ON NEW 'BORGMOBILE.'

SUBJECT IS ATTEMPTING TO RETRIEVE BARBECUE UNIT FROM THE COLLECTIVE.
HOW IS HE NOT BURNING HIS HANDS?
AND I'M KEEPING THE BURGERS INSIDE IT.
TWO OF FOUR WANTED A HOT DOG.

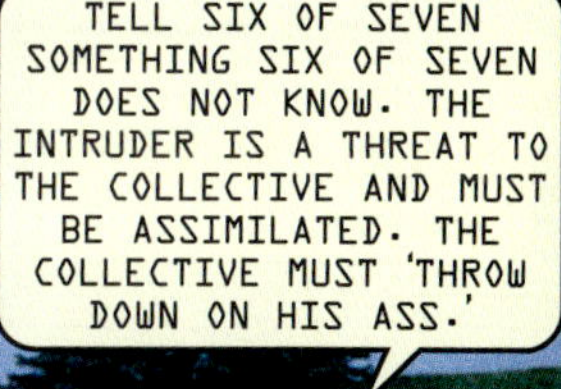
TELL SIX OF SEVEN SOMETHING SIX OF SEVEN DOES NOT KNOW. THE INTRUDER IS A THREAT TO THE COLLECTIVE AND MUST BE ASSIMILATED. THE COLLECTIVE MUST 'THROW DOWN ON HIS ASS.'

WE ARE BORG. RESISTANCE IS--

TEACH THEM TO--HEY, I USED TO HAVE MORE YARD THAN THIS! THOSE LITTLE GRAY BASTARDS...!

I OUGHTA-- WHAT THE--?!?

GET YOUR PASTY BALD ASS OFF OF MY ROOF!
NEGATIVE. THIS TELEVISION RECEPTOR MUST BE ASSIMILATED. THE COLLECTIVE DESIRES 'BAYWATCH' FIVE NIGHTS A WEEK. AND UNIT IS 'FAIR SKINNED,' NOT 'PASTY.'

DONNA D'ERRICO MUST BE ASSIMILATED BY THIS UNIT PERSONALLY. SHE--

SPLOOSH!!

AND STAY OFF, OR NEXT TIME I'LL GET THE RAKE!!!

AND THAT'S THAT. I WONDER IF 'BUFFY' IS ON... *HEY!!!*

YOU'RE LUCKY THERE WAS NO GLASS IN THAT WINDOW. AND PUT MY TOASTER DOWN!
NEGATIVE. THE COLLECTIVE DESIRES CRISP, CRUNCHY BAGELS EACH MORNING.

I WOULDN'T MIND IF IT WAS THAT TOP-HEAVY CHICK FROM 'VOYAGER,' BUT THESE GUYS ARE GETTIN' REALLY ANNOYING.

FIVE OF SIXTEEN HAS ASSIMILATED A TEAPOT.
ELEVEN OF THREE HAS ASSIMILATED A LAMP.
'TENNIS, ANYONE?' NINE OF SIX HAS ASSIMILATED COMEDY.

BEANIE BABY TAGS? THREE OF TWENTY FEELS NAUSEOUS.
FOUR OF FOUR FEELS PRETTY.
I ALMOST FEEL BAD DOING THIS, BUT YOU'VE GOT IT COMING AFTER THAT LAST CRAPPY 'TREK' MOVIE.

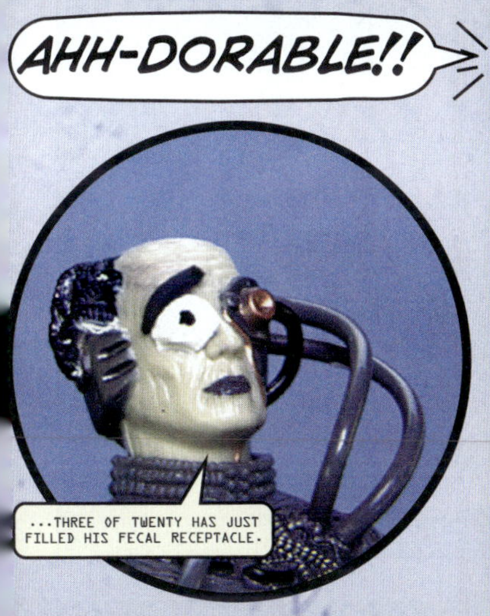
AHH-DORABLE!!
...THREE OF TWENTY HAS JUST FILLED HIS FECAL RECEPTACLE.

THESE MUST BE THE NEW BEANIES!
OH MY GAWD...THEY'RE PRECIOUS!
PROBABLY FROM LONG ISLAND.
YENTAS!!!

NINE OF TWO IS BORG! NINE OF TWO IS NOT 'COLLECTIBLE'!
THE ODINSON HATH HOSES WHERE HE WOULD PREFER HOSES NOT BE.
TOO MUCH INFORMATION.
THREE OF FOURTEEN! CAN SEVEN OF EIGHT HAVE YOUR RECORD COLLECTION?
THREE OF FOURTEEN THOUGHT THIS TYPE OF THING ONLY HAPPENED IN THE PENTHOUSE LETTERS PAGE.
MINE'S NAME IS PEANUT!
THE END

THE BORG

Height: 6 inches
Weight: 1.9 oz.
Representatives: 4 of 5, 11 of 3, 25 or 6 to 4
Method of Transportation: Giant metal crouton
First Appearance: "The New Neighbors," *ToyFare* #14
Died: "Kirks Up, Ho's Down," *ToyFare* #112
History: It is unknown how many Borg moved in next door to Spider-Man in *ToyFare* #14—nor what strategic importance that particular Megoville neighborhood held—but their unified purpose drove them towards a single goal: steal Spider-Man's stuff. While most of the items stolen seemed to be purely for entertainment purposes, it has been assumed that Spidey's quick action with a hose and subsequent "tagging" of the Borg infestation saved Earth from some sinister Borg threat. So powerful was Spider-Man's defeat of the Borg that he later enlisted them to fight on the side of the angels during the Crisis on Infinite Megovilles, where a motley group of characters banded together to deprive an old lady of her oven mitt (*ToyFare* #75). They would return to their evil ways, however, when they threatened the crew of the *Enterprise D* in *ToyFare* #112, not knowing that Captain James T. Kirk was on board. Kirk quickly routed them, preying on the feminine weaknesses of the Borg Queen and taking her severed head for a bride.
Powers: The Borg are able to assimilate any race into their techno-organic hive mind. Also, they can formulate an attack that will breach any defense and a defense to repel any attack; as a result, it is very difficult to win an argument against them.

TOYFARE #14 "The New Neighbors"

TOYFARE #112 "Kirk's Up, Ho's Down"

A Real American Hero

As originally published in *ToyFare* #40

"I think before this sketch we were relying too much on the fact that, 'Oh, Iron Man is drunk. What will he do this installment? He'll be drunk again!' And we said, 'How can we do something else beyond that?' We really tried to explore comedy from other characters beyond the superheroes and bring them into the fold."

- Doug Goldstein

"I seem to remember some hesitation about using the Uncle Ben ending to this one. I think that not all the writers agreed that turning the strip into *Amazing Fantasy* #15 was the right way to end our slam-bang G.I. Joe adventure. But I freakin' loved it, and I still do."

- Tom Root

Twisted ToyFare Theatre

A Real American Hero

By Pat McCallum, Tom Root and Douglas Goldstein

Photos by Paul Schiraldi.

SUDDENLY...
COOOOOBBBRRRAAA!!
BRAAAAA, BRA, BRA, BRA!
HEE-HEE.

THE GAME ISSS AFOOT!
THISSS DAY MARKSSS THE TURNING POINT, ASSS I-- COBRA COMMANDER-- FINALLY GAIN THE UPPER HAND ON THE WRETCHED G.I. JOE...
... AND THE WORLD!

YOU ARE SO PAYING FOR THAT WALL!
SSSILENCE! NONE SHALL SSSTAND BETWEEN COBRA AND GLORY!
REVEREND!
REVEREND!

BESSSIDES, HOW DO WE KNOW ZART--I MEAN--THISSS SSSPIDER-MAN ISSSN'T THE REAL SSSPIDER-MAN?
HELLO, MY NAME IS SPIDER-MAN. PLEASE MAKE A HOLE IN MY WALL!
...SSSEE?

HOLY -HUUUURP- COW! I'LL HAFTA KILL Y'BOTH T' BE SURE!
I HEAR YOU SLOSHING. GO EMPTY YOUR ARMOR.
REDRUM! REDRUM!

NOW, WHILE THEY'RE DISSSTRACTED! DESSSTRO, MAJOR BLUDD--SSSPLIT UP AND LOCATE THAT WHICH WE SSSEEK!
FINAL VICTORY SHALL BE OURS!
WHO'S DOING WHAT NOW?

SUDDENLY...
YOOOO, JOE!
FIGHTING FOR FREEDOM OVER LAND AND AIR!
UUURP! UH-OH! BATS!
...AND THEY'RE PARACHUTING IN FROM WHERE, EXACTLY?

KILL 'EM ALL AND LET GOD SORT 'EM OUT, BOYS!
EAT THEIR HEARTSSS AND SSSPIT BLOOD AT THEIR WIDOWSSS!
...WHAT?

THIS URP THIS ALWAYS HAPPENS WHEN I'M DRINKING.
SO THIS IS WHAT REAGAN'S AMERICA WAS LIKE.
ICE CREAM
YO JOE!
COBRA!

...THEY'LL STAY 'TIL THE FIGHT'S WON, G.I. JOE IS THERE...
BLAST! NOW THAT SONG WILL BE IN MY HEAD FOR WEEKS!
BAH! THE MISSION WILL SUCCEED REGAR--
I ♥ NY

CLINK! CLINK! CLINK!
GAH! STUPID METAL HEAD!
I ♥ NY
THOK!

AWAY! STAY AWAY, YOU FETID BOOZEHOUND!
I -URP- NEED THAT BOTTLE OPENER! OTHERWISE, TH' BEER WON'T COME OUT!

TELEVIPERSSS! ESSSTABLISH A SSSECURE LINE OF COMMUNICATION BETWEEN--
I HAVE A NAME, AND IT'S DAVE. THIS IS CORY.
HI.

HELLO, THIS IS SPIDER-MAN. PLEASE DELIVER FORTY-THREE ANCHOVY PIZZAS TO MY HOUSE.
AND A CHERRY COKE.
WHAT ARE YOU, IN FOURTH GRADE? GIMME THAT!
HEY! MINE!
Lay's Potato Chips
THE TELEPHONE IS A PRIVILEGE, NOT A RIGHT, KIDS.
AND KNOWING IS HALF THE BATTLE!
...WHAT'S THE OTHER HALF?
Lay's Potato Chips

...VIOLENCE.
EHH, HEH-HEH-HEH!

ZAP!
BANG!
BLAM!
BLAM!
BANG!
Lay's Potato Chips

LOWER. ONE OF YOU GUYS MIGHT ACTUALLY HIT SOMETHING IF YOU AIM LOWER.
HEY!
BLAM!
AIEEE...
Lay's Potato Chips

DUDE, THAT'S...THAT'S NOT HOW WE PLAY.
...MONSTER.
FRANK? FRANK?!?
Lay's Potato Chips

SSSUCCESSSS!
WITH YOUR UNCLE BEN'SSS ASHESSS, THE WORLD'SSS MOSSST SSSINISTER SSSCIENTIFIC MINDSSS HAVE ENGINEERED THE ULTIMATE MILITARY LEADER...
Lay's Potato Chips

I... LIVE.
...BEN SSSERPENTOR!
MAZEL-TOV!

OKAY, **NOW** TODAY IS OFFICIALLY THE WEIRDEST DAY EVER.

MY LOYAL FOLLOWERS, **HEED THESE WORDS...**
...EAT YOUR WHEATCAKES!
WHAT'S A WHEATCAKE?

HEY!
STOP THAT BURGLAR!

BLAM!
URK!

...ALL YOU HAD TO DO WAS **TRIP** HIM OR SOMETHING...
HAVE YOU NO SENSE OF RESPONSIBILITY?
IT'S BETTER THIS WAY. HE WAS INCONTINENT.
'EAT YOUR WHEATCAKESSS'? I WOULD'VE SHOT HIM **MYSSSELF!**
END

COBRA

TOYFARE #65 "The Cold War"

History: No one knows from whence Cobra came. Some say it was founded by a race of snake-people who live in the Arctic, but most people tend to ignore that notion. Instead, most believe that a former used-car salesman teamed up with a Scottish, metal-masked arms dealer, an Australian biker gang and a shirtless orthodontist to form one of the most lethal terrorist organizations known to mankind.

Appearances: After their debut in *ToyFare* #40, the diminutive forces of Cobra were discovered still living in the walls of Spider-Man's house in "The Cold War" (*ToyFare* #65). Despite their having recently resurrected his dead uncle, Spider-Man allowed them to stay in exchange for paying rent, chipping in for groceries and cleaning out the gutters. Cobra would move onto bigger and better living quarters by *ToyFare* #74, when they were seen living in the Terrordrome, which is apparently a kind of drome. It was from this location that they launched such doomed missions as the parade of *ToyFare* #80, which was cancelled due to permit issues. Finally, after the destruction of their giant sea serpent (*ToyFare* #109), their next step was to convert the Terrordrome into a fast-food restaurant called the Burger Drome. It would be their most successful (and fattening) campaign ever, and it would lead to the rise of a new Cobra Leader, the Burger Meister. Cobra Commander, reduced to dressing in a giant hot dog suit, now has nothing else to do but play *Risk* with his other 1980s cartoon buddies at Gargamel's house (*ToyFare* #82).

COBRA COMMANDER

Although he prefers to wear this metal face-plate, also has a soft fabric hood that doubles as a napkin.

DESTRO

Looks a lot like Steve Guttenberg under his mask, which explains why he rarely removes it.

BARONESS

There are dozens of obscene stories about this Eastern European noblewoman floating around the Cobra motor pool. 75% of them are true.

DR. MINDBENDER

Formerly an orthodontist, Mindbender now gets his jollies by making cups of coffee obscenely hot.

BURGER MEISTER

Formed by combining the DNA of some of the fast food industry's greatest mascots, the Burger Meister has a keen business sense. And a crown.

SPIDER-MAN

The true identity of Cobra's tiny Spider-Man is unknown, but he is responsible for the delivery of a large number of pizzas to Spidey's house.

THE TENTH ANNIVERSARY STRIP

HOT THESPIAN ACTION

It wouldn't be a celebration of our tenth anniversary without acknowledging one simple fact: we still got it! Damn! Our skillz are off the hizook for realz! Bearing that in mind, we wanted to do more in this book than just present you with the most memorable moments of our past—we wanted to show you the future. The following strip was created for and will be available exclusively in this volume. So enjoy, and keep reading "Twisted ToyFare Theatre"!

Twisted ToyFare Theatre PRESENTS

HOT Thespian Action!

BY: ACLIN, OAT & GUTIERREZ WITH: COLLINS & WARD

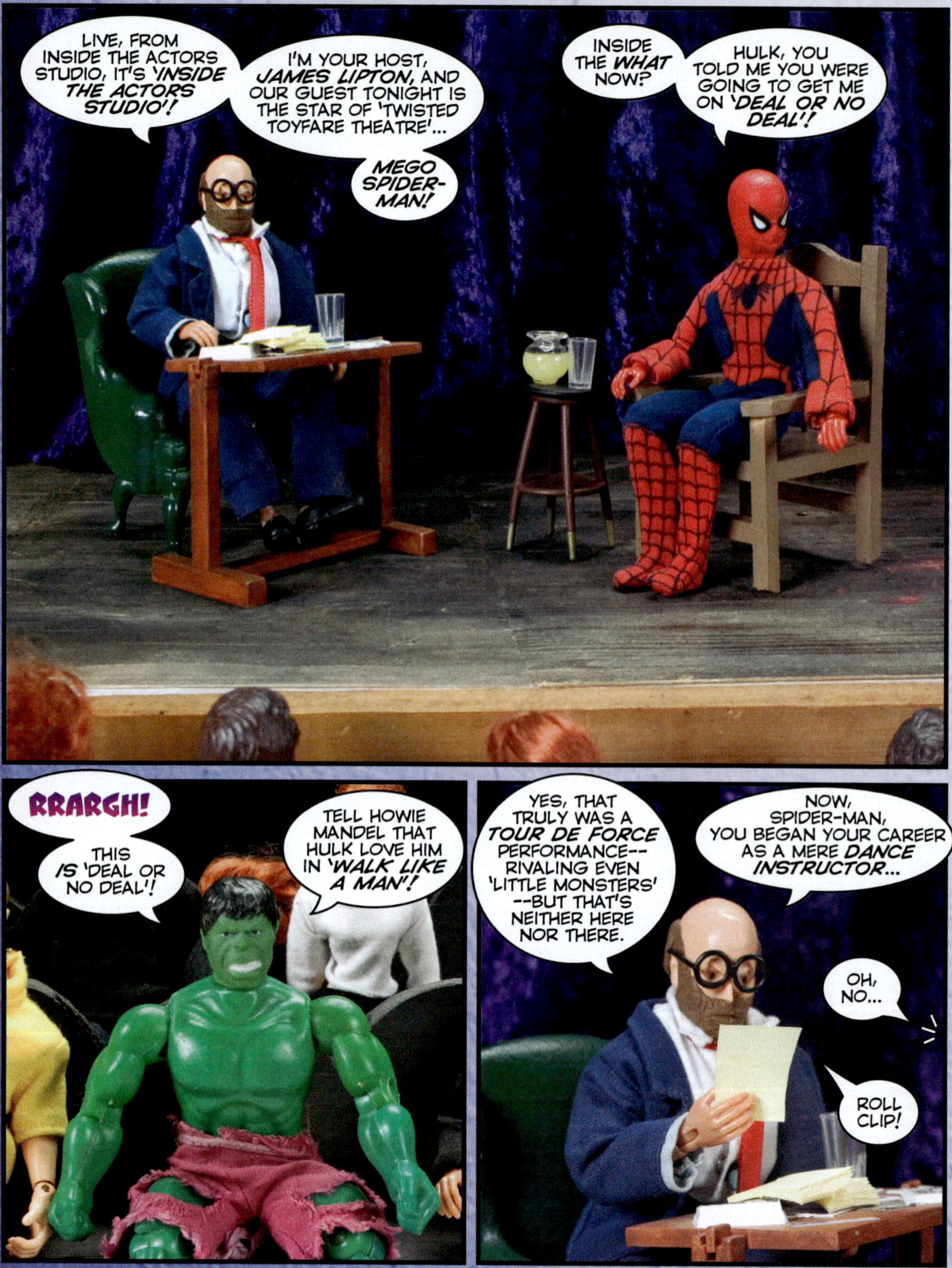

LIVE, FROM INSIDE THE ACTORS STUDIO, IT'S *'INSIDE THE ACTORS STUDIO'!*

I'M YOUR HOST, *JAMES LIPTON,* AND OUR GUEST TONIGHT IS THE STAR OF 'TWISTED TOYFARE THEATRE'...

MEGO SPIDER-MAN!

INSIDE THE *WHAT* NOW?

HULK, YOU TOLD ME YOU WERE GOING TO GET ME ON *'DEAL OR NO DEAL'!*

FROM THE 'TOYFARE' WINTER SPECIAL

FROM 'TOYFARE' #3

FROM 'TOYFARE' #5

FROM 'TOYFARE' #25

THEN, YOUR CAREER A SHAMBLES, YOU WERE LEFT WITH NO CHOICE BUT TO ENTER THE PORNOGRAPHY INDUSTRY.
NO PUN INTENDED.
PORN?
I HOPE I'D REMEMBER IF I--

I ART THE LAST BOY! I ART THE LAST BOY!!
...GREAT. NOW I'M IN A 'THREE'S COMPANY' EPISODE.
FROM 'TOYFARE' #28

SPIDER-MAN... WHEN DID YOU REALIZE THAT YOU WERE A SHAMELESS PROSTITUTE?
HEY... THAT PANEL WAS TOTALLY TAKEN OUT OF CONTEXT!
VERY WELL... LET'S SHOW THE PANEL BEFORE IT.

SUDDENLY...
CLICK!

YES, NOW YOU ARE TRULY VINDICATED.
YOU DON'T HAVE TO BE A DICK ABOUT IT!
FINALLY, YOU STRETCHED YOUR ACTING MUSCLES WHEN YOU APPEARED AS 'MEXICAN SPIDER-MAN.'

ADONDE ESTA EL PESCADO, BURRITO, BURRITO, BURRITO?*
*WE ARE OFF TO THE BEACH TO PLAY LOUD MUSIC.
FROM 'TOYFARE' #33.

MAY I... SPEAK TO MEXICAN SPIDER-MAN?
UH, NO THANKS, THAT SOUNDS--

OH, I WASN'T ASKING...
HEY... WHAT'RE YOU--

DON'T BOTHER TRYING TO SHAKE THEM OFF, SPIDER-MAN... I BELIEVE YOU'LL FIND THE ADHESIVE IS QUITE STRONG.
HULK, GET ME OUT OF HERE!
NO DEAL!

AND NOW WE COME TO YOUR GREATEST AND FINAL ROLE... AS A VICTIM OF MY METHOD MACHINE, WHICH DRAINS ACTORS OF THEIR EMOTIONS AND GIVES THEM TO MY STUDENTS!
WE ALREADY HAVE THE RAW SEXUALITY OF THE YOUNG MARLON BRANDO, THE GRACE OF AUDREY HEPBURN AND THE CRAZY EYES OF MARTY FELDMAN.

"BUT FIRST...I BELIEVE THAT ROBERT HAD A QUESTION TO ASK YOU."
HI, SPIDER-MAN-- I'M A BIG FAN...
THEN HOW ABOUT SAVING MY LIFE?
...AND I WAS WONDERING-- WHAT'S YOUR FAVORITE WORD?
WHAT?

THAT'S MY LINE!
NOBODY MAY ASK THE QUESTIONS OF BERNARD PIVOT BUT ME!
BLAM!
BLAM!
URK!

LET'S JUST SKIP TO THE FINAL QUESTION...
WHAT DO YOU WANT TO HEAR ST. PETER SAY WHEN YOU APPROACH THE PEARLY GATES...
...30 SECONDS FROM NOW?
UH...

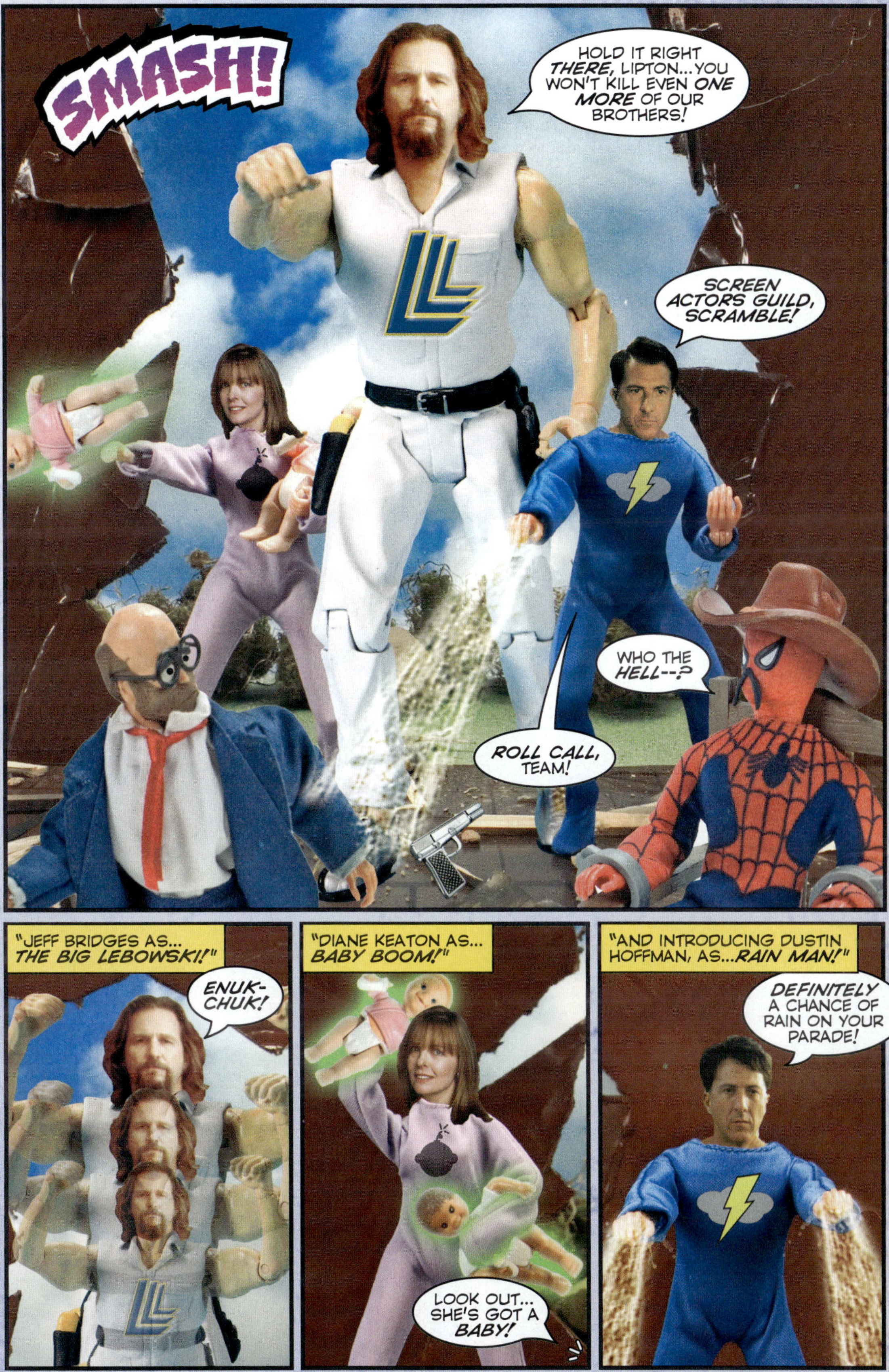

SMASH!

HOLD IT RIGHT *THERE,* LIPTON...YOU WON'T KILL EVEN *ONE MORE* OF OUR BROTHERS!

SCREEN ACTORS GUILD, SCRAMBLE!

WHO THE *HELL--?*

ROLL CALL, TEAM!

DESTROY THEM, MY STUDENTS!
YOU *WILL* BE GRADED ON THIS!
FSSH!
CLICK!

I'M...IN... *PAIN!*
BOOM!
WHAT'S MY MOTIVA-- *URK!*

BOOM!
THIS SEEMS LIKE A GOOD TIME TO *GET THE HELL OUT OF HERE* AND FORGET THIS EVER HAPPENED.
AIEE!
EXIT
HOP!
HOP!

PHEW!
NOW HOW DO I GET OUT OF THIS *ALLEY?*
NO RE-ENTRY
SLAM!

AIN'T NO WAY OUTTA THIS ALLEY.
I'VE BEEN HERE FOR *YEARS,* LIVING OFF THE FOOD THE ACTORS WON'T EAT FOR *MORAL REASONS.*
WELL, WHAT THE HELL AM I SUPPOSED TO *DO?*

SOON...
WELCOME TO 'OUTSIDE THE ACTORS STUDIO,' WHERE MY GUEST TODAY IS A MEXICAN GENTLEMAN TIED TO A CHAIR.
RRARGH!
BUY VOWEL!
SHUT UP!
END

THE CREATION OF A 'TTT'

Was that strip you just read hilarious or what? But we bet you're asking yourself, "How does the *ToyFare* staff do it? Does it involve magic and goat sacrifice or simply technology from the future?" It's actually neither! Each "TTT" strip simply starts with an idea. In this case, the idea was "Let's do an *Inside the Actors Studio* parody so we can do a clip show and save ourselves a lot of work." So how did we get from there to a super-powered Dustin Hoffman? Read on to find out...

MEETING OF THE MINDS From left: Zach, Jon and Justin argue the finer points of fart jokes in the initial outline meeting.

Once the idea is decided, an email goes out to all the "Twisted ToyFare" writers asking for ideas for specific gags. Some of them make it into the final strip—"Random idea," Zach Oat wrote, "Who would host 'Outside the Actors Studio?' Is it James Lipton, or some crazy bum?"

Other ideas plant a seed but don't make it. "Maybe at the end the *E! True Hollywood Story* crew shows up to do a profile on Spidey, and James Lipton gets all indignant because they're interrupting his class, so a brawl breaks out," wrote Justin Aclin. Other ideas simply never make it into the strip; suggested alternate hosts besides James Lipton included Dr. Strange, William Shatner and homeless superhero D-Man.

With all the ideas collected, the core writing staff (Justin Aclin, Zach Oat and Jon Gutierrez) head into a conference room and start talking. This is where the true meat of every strip is hashed out, where an off-the-cuff comment can change the entire course of a strip. And if you were a fly on the wall, you would have heard a lot of bad James Lipton impressions, and this...

ACLIN: So Sean [Collins] seems to be of the opinion that it shouldn't be James Lipton at all, or even a James Lipton-esque character.

OAT: He says that James Lipton has been parodied a bunch of times and I will admit that I'm kind of worried we're going to be in the shadow of Will Ferrell.

ACLIN: I feel like every James Lipton parody I've seen the actor's been very game with it, like they're playing into this whole ego thing that he does. Where as Spider-Man is going to be bewildered by the whole thing. So how does Spider-Man get roped into this?

OAT: I like someone's suggestion of the Hulk thinking he was getting him onto *Deal or No Deal*.

GUTIERREZ: That would be the one game show Spidey would go on 'cause it's the laziest game show. You just pick a case, and that's it.

OAT: So Spider-Man's at a studio, he's like, "I've got these *Deal or No Deal* tickets and I can't find the studio," or something like that. And he goes through the wrong door and he's on stage. And James Lipton's like, "Spider-Man, our next guest!"

ACLIN: Or maybe Hulk just actually does think this is *Deal or No Deal*. "Rrargh, Howie Mandel make Hulk laugh!"

OAT: "Hulk love Howie Mandel in *Walk Like Man*!"

GUTIERREZ: "I think you're missing his tour de force performance as Gizmo in *Gremlins*."

OAT: Do you think it's worth it to have some sort of set-up before he gets to the stage? Like backstage or like at home with Spider-Man? Or do you think we should just start off on the show?

GUTIERREZ: I think we'll be able to get enough out of the show that we don't need it.

ACLIN: "You started your career as a dance instructor..."

OAT: "Oh, God." Spider-Man should just...every other panel he should have his hands on his forehead.

GUTIERREZ: "Did you allow the Latin rhythms to invade your body?"

ACLIN: "You followed this tour de force...with an infomercial."

GUTIERREZ: "You worked with Mr. T."

ACLIN: "Spider-Man, why were you afraid to let your acting muscles...flex?"

GUTIERREZ: "Are you coming onto me?" "No...but do the Macarena."

ACLIN: "Then you appeared in a *Scream* parody with Fonzie."

OAT: I don't know, is this strip even worth mentioning? I mean, I know it's embarrassing, but I wonder if there's a joke that can even be made about it. "Have you ever given any thought to the ending of what this strip meant?" And Spider-Man's like, "I have no idea what that meant."

ACLIN: What if it's like, "Let us watch." And they show a couple panels. And they cut back and James Lipton's like, "Now, Spider-Man, how did it feel to work with Henry Wink–" And Spider-Man's not there. And James Lipton goes, "It's not going to be that easy. Guards!" And they come and they drag Spider-Man back.

GUTIERREZ: *That's* pretty funny.

OAT: "All the doors of the Actors Studio are guarded by trained ac-tors!"

GUTIERREZ: Trained to act like armed guards.

ACLIN: "Spider-Man, in your performance in that escape attempt, did you really feel like you could get away? Because there is no escape."

OAT: Does he just slowly reveal himself to be more and more evil and megalomaniacal?

GUTIERREZ: That's an approach no one's taken.

ACLIN: "We will watch the most horrid moments of your career, and there is no escape."

GUTIERREZ: "And then you discovered that I had your Aunt May, being tortured in a small room in the back."

ACLIN: That's pretty funny... When they put Spidey back in the chair, do shackles come over his arms?

OAT: When he sits down again? "Spider-Man, you've forfeited the trust that we placed in you here Inside the Actors Studio."

ACLIN: So, where's it going at this point? Is he just torturing Spider-Man?

OAT: Yes. He's figuratively torturing him and he's also beginning to literally torture him.

ACLIN: I like this set-up but I'm not sure where to take it from here.

OAT: I think we take six strips that we can get the funniest jokes out of that really show some sort of progress to Spider-Man's career.

ACLIN: So we've got him as a dance instructor, hosting info-mercials...

OAT: Game-show host.

ACLIN: ...in the *Scream* parody... We could do the adult film thing we were talking about...

OAT: I think the Mexican one is a funny one to do, because it's like him trying to stretch his skills as an actor. Oh, but this strip is in the book.

ACLIN: That's okay. We'll just show one panel from it. I do think it would be funny if he said, "Can I...speak to Mexican Spider-Man?"

GUTIERREZ: And having one of the guys come out with a sarape and hat and a mustache.

ACLIN: And Spider-Man just looks at him blankly and one of the guards comes out with that and he goes, "...That wasn't a question."

OAT: Should Spider-Man somewhere say, "Hulk, will you please help me here?" And Hulk should yell something about a completely different game show. Hulk could be like, "Rrargh! Pick center square!"

GUTIERREZ: Or if Spidey calls for help he could be like, "Hulk no speak Spanish! What you say?"

OAT: I'm trying to think how to elevate this and how to give Spider-Man the opportunity to escape.

GUTIERREZ: What if they reveal that Lipton's a serial killer. He's been doing this to actors for a while and there's like a pile of actors lying there?

OAT: He's just surrounded by bodies?

GUTIERREZ: All wearing sombreros and mustaches.

DRAWN AND QUARTERED Zach Oat's storyboards show the photographers exactly what to shoot and which toys need googly eyes.

VILLAINS, INC. Photographer Dylan Brucie takes Zach's storyboards, a closet full of Megos and a bunch of little white clay eyes and crafts the raw visual materials we'll turn into the finished products.

IS GOOD! Lead "TTT" designer Eric Goodman takes the photos and adds word balloons, Photoshop effects and, often, new heads (like the celebrity heads on the Screen Actor's Guild). It's a lot of work, but we keep him medicated.

ACLIN: We could elevate it just by James Lipton saying, "And then came your final role...as a victim of my Method Machine. Where I drain all your emotions and use it to fuel my acting students' abilities."

OAT: "I now possess the facial expressions of Jack Nicholson, the sullen demeanor of Robert DeNiro..."

GUTIERREZ: "The quiet innocence of John Ritter..."

OAT: And then who intervenes? Does S.H.I.E.L.D. bust in?

GUTIERREZ: Are we missing a chance to have somebody ask a question like they typically do on Actors Studio?

ACLIN: Definitely before the escalation, he could be like, "But before you die, let me just ask you, when you get to Heaven, what would you like to hear St. Peter say?"

OAT: "Congratulations, you're the first person to be crushed by models."

ACLIN: What if one of the students asks him, "Spider-Man, what's your favorite word?" And Lipton goes, "I ASK THAT!" and shoots lasers out of his hand?

OAT: Blue lightning. "Yaaaah!" ...So how does Spider-Man escape?

ACLIN: Well now that he's shot blue lightning, do we do a bit of an Emperor riff, where he's got a gun at his side and Spidey's looking at it? "You...want this?"

OAT: Rather than going the Star Wars route with the lightning is it funnier if he just pulls out a Luger and shoots him, so he's more of a Bond villain than a Star Wars villain? I mean...'cause the lightning is funny, visually. James Lipton using lightning to kill a kid. But I wonder if him just pulling out a Luger—BLAM—and then just putting it on a desk...

ACLIN: "And now, the final curtain." Which, of course, I stole from Sideshow Bob.

OAT: Well, Jon seems to like the S.H.I.E.L.D. thing coming in. Is that...I feel like there needs to be some sort of distraction for Spider-Man to hop out the door and Hulk doesn't seem at all interested in providing it.

ACLIN: I feel like...and I hope I'm not just sticking to it because it's my idea, but I feel like whatever opposing force comes in also has to be entertainment-based. Like maybe not the *E! True Hollywood Story* crew but something...

GUTIERREZ: The Screen Actors Guild...

OAT: The Screen Actors Guild comes through the wall and they're all superheroes!

GUTIERREZ: Could the Screen Actors Guild be actors in superhero versions of their famous roles? Like Jeff Bridges as the Big Lebowski, and he's like an Apache Chief?

ACLIN: "Screen Actors Guild roll call! Jeff Bridges as the Big Lebowski!"

OAT: "Enuk Chuk!"

ACLIN: Dustin Hoffman as Rain Man?

OAT: And, uh...Melanie Griffith as Working Girl!

ACLIN: Diane Keaton as Baby Boom.

OAT: Boom! She's throwing babies who explode at people! These are obviously the first three actors that came to mind. I'm sure if we thought about it we could come up with better actors. Like...Peter Fonda as Easy Rider.

GUTIERREZ: Tom Cruise as Top Gun.

ACLIN: Matthew McConaughey as the Rain Maker! Who's sorta...redundant.

OAT: "I was very influenced by Dustin Hoffman."

ACLIN: Well, what's James Lipton's countermeasure? He has to have some sort of countermeasure.

OAT: "You can't defeat me, I have the power of Robin Williams!"

ACLIN: "You should have never confronted me on my home turf. Or have you forgotten, we are inside...the Actors Studio!" And then, like, spikes come out of the ceiling.

OAT: Lasers blasts and robot arms with buzzsaws and stuff like that. It's like the Danger Room.

ACLIN: [*Laughs.*] You know...this turned into something very, very different. **TF**

From the Vault

"Twisted ToyFare Theatre" proved so popular that it was quickly stolen for use in other Wizard Entertainment products. These special-edition magazines and "ACE Edition" comic books were seldom seen by *ToyFare* fans, and so they are among the rarest specimens of "TTT" in existence. Collected in this section you will find four such strips—"White Trash Talkin'" from the *Uncanny X-Men* #94 ACE Edition, "Galactic Chef" from the *Fantastic Four* #48 ACE Edition, "Four Webbings and a Funeral" from the *Wizard Spider-Man Special*, and "Bathroom Blitz," which was intended to be included in an *Amazing Spider-Man* #1 ACE Edition but was left out at the last minute and has never been seen before by human eyes (the "Twisted ToyFare" production staff being robots).

Twisted ToyFare Theatre
PRESENTS
WHITE TRASH TALKIN'
...AND WELCOME BACK TO THE JERRY SPRINGER SHOW.
IF YOU'RE JUST JOINING US, OUR GUEST IS THE X-MAN KNOW AS CYCLOPS. IS HE THE PATRIACH OF A LOVEABLE DYSFUNCTIONAL MUTANT FAMILY OR A BLOODTHIRSTY MUTANT AFTER OUR WOMEN?
YOU DECIDE!
I'M A WHAT NOW?

"JOINING US FIRST, CYCLOPS' RESURRECTED WIFE, JEAN GREY."
THIS BETTER BE QUICK...I FEEL THE PHOENIX FORVE GROWING INSIDE ME.
I HUNGER...
...THIS IS DIFFERENT FROM AUNT FLO, RIGHT?

"AND VIA SATELLITE FROM THE SHI'AR EMPIRE, CYCLOPS' FATHER, THE SPACE PIRATE CORSAIR."
ARRR, ME BOY IS A MENACE! HE SENT ME GRANDSON INTO AN APOCALYPTIC FUTURE!
WHAT WOULD YUR MUDDAH SAY?

WHAT?!? YOU DUMPED MOM FOR AN ALIEN SKUNK GIRL AND PUSHED ME OUT OF A PLANE!
WHEN I WAS LIKE FIVE!

YOU HAVE SOMETHING YOU WANT TO SAY?
JEANNIE, YOU SHOULD DROP DAT BUM AND GET WITH ME! I'LL TREAT YOU RIGHT!

YOU SHUT UP!
AT LEAST I'M AN AMERICAN CITIZEN, MR. JOHNNY NO GREEN CARD.
HEY, AT LEAST I DIDN'T LAUNCH MY KID INTO SPACE.

AND WHAT OF YOUR OTHER CHILDREN, CYCLOPS?
A DAUGHTER CONCEIVED BY A PARALLEL DIMENSION SCOTT SUMMERS, A.K.A....YOU?

OH THAT'S JUST PERFECT! WERE YOU EVER GOING TO TELL ME?!?
WHAT?!? THAT WASN'T ME, THAT WAS DIFFERENT ME FROM A DIFFERENT DIMEN--WHO THE?
MR. SINISTER?
WHAT'S UP CHI-CA-GO!

COMING UP AFTER THE BREAK, MUTANTS: THREAT TO HUMANITY OR GOOD EATIN'?
HEY... SPARE ANY DNA SAMPLES?
I, UH... I DON'T SWING THAT WAY.
END

Twisted ToyFare Theatre
"...GALACTUS, MARINADER OF WORLDS!"
I'M WILLIAM SHATNER, AND WELCOME TO IRON CHEF U.S.A!
IF MEMORY SERVES ME, MY IRON CHEF JAPANESE MASAHARU MORIMOTO FACES A CHALLENGER WHO IS NO STRANGER TO EXOTIC DELICACIES...
PAM GETS GREASE OUT OF GALACTUS' WAY.
STUPID WORLD-EATING GAIJIN.
GALACTIC CHEF
BY MCCALLUM, OAT, ACLIN & BRICKEN

"TODAY'S SECRET INGREDIENT, BEING UNVEILED BY IRON CHEFS KIKI AND SUMMER IS..."

"...THE SKRULL HOMEWORLD!"
FWOOSH!
THE SUN! THE SUN IS BACK!
OH THANK GOODNESS!
WAIT...WHERE ARE WE?

G...GRANDMA?
HAW!
SHAPESHIFT YER WAY OUTTA DIS ONE, UGLY.

"LET THE COMPETITION BEGIN!"
THOUGH I AM SWORN NEVER TO INTERFERE, THIS SOUP NEEDS MORE PAPRIKA...

HEY!
SHOULDN'T YOU BE OFF HOSTING A 'WHAT IF?' SOMEWHERE?
SCRAM!
JUST A DASH!

"SOMETHING'S HAPPENING OVER WITH THE CHALLENGER'S ASSISTANT..."
WITH THE POWER COSMIC I'VE STOLEN FROM THE SILVER SURFER, I SHALL LAUNCH ALL BUILDINGS INTO SPACE!
SPACE!
FZZZZZZZZZT!

"AND AS THE TIME LIMIT EXPIRES, IRON CHEF JAPANESE HAS FIVE DISHES PREPARED, INCLUDING SKRULL HOMEWORLD AU GRATIN AND SKRULL BITS WITH FOIS GRAS!"
AND HERE'S A LITTLE SOMETHING EXTRA FOR EVERYONE WHO STEPS UP TO MORIMOTO!

"AND ON THE CHALLENGER'S SIDE, WE HAVE...NOTHING."
I...I HUNGERED...
BRAP!

IRON CHEF JAPANESE WINS AGAIN!
TUNE IN NEXT WEEK AS OUR IRON CHEF GERMAN FACES HIS TOUGHEST CHALLENGE YET...WITH A VERY SPECIAL INGREDIENT!
RELAX, SOLDIER-- MY ROCKY MOUNTAIN OYSTERS RECIPE HASN'T FAILED ME YET!
NEIN! I'M GOINK TO STUFF YOU VIT DAS SAUSAGE DER HARD VAY!
NOT AGAIN...!
END

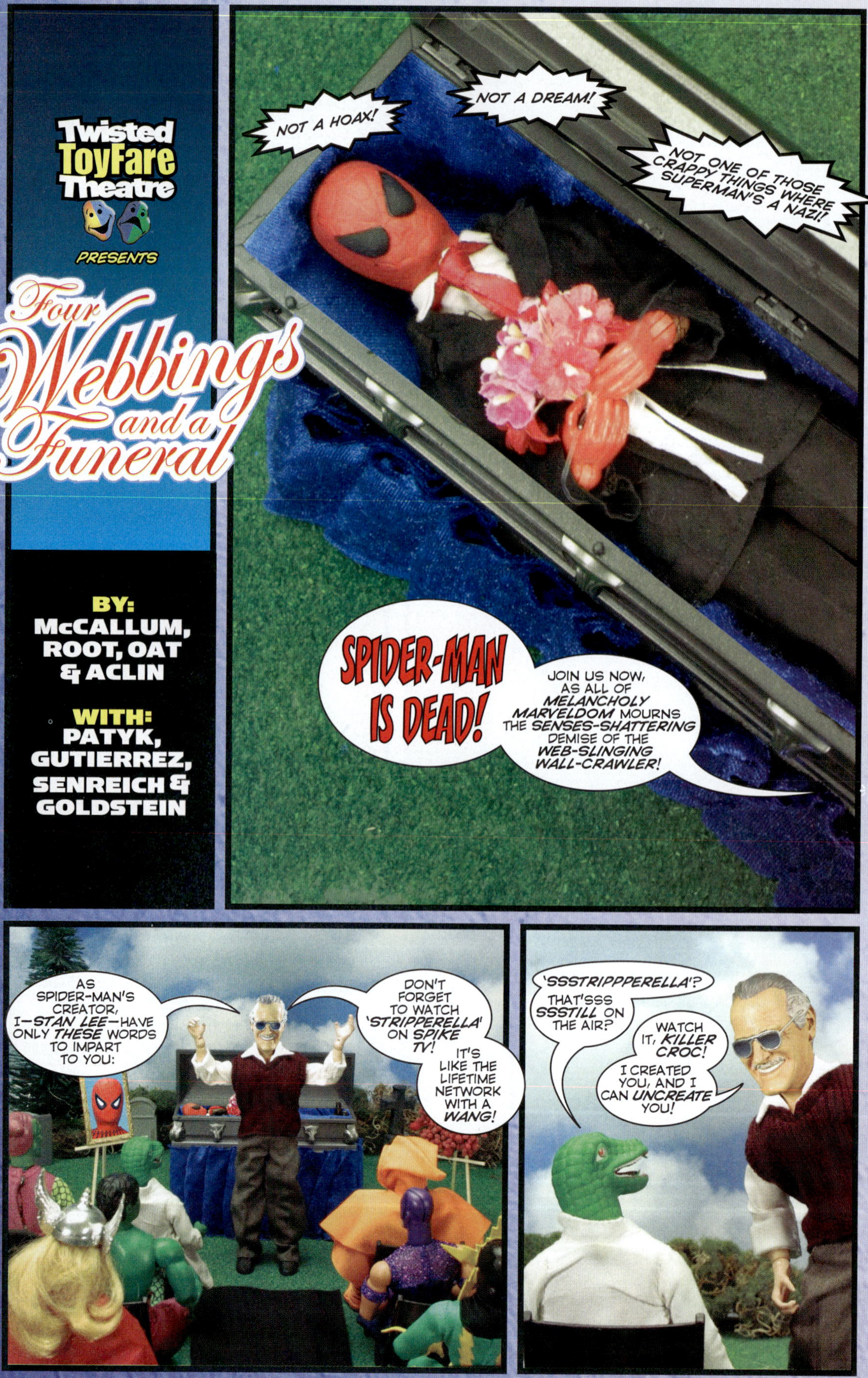

Twisted ToyFare Theatre

PRESENTS

Four Webbings and a Funeral

BY: McCALLUM, ROOT, OAT & ACLIN

WITH: PATYK, GUTIERREZ, SENREICH & GOLDSTEIN

NOT A HOAX!

NOT A DREAM!

NOT ONE OF THOSE CRAPPY THINGS WHERE SUPERMAN'S A NAZI!!

SPIDER-MAN IS DEAD!

JOIN US NOW, AS ALL OF *MELANCHOLY MARVELDOM* MOURNS THE *SENSES-SHATTERING* DEMISE OF THE *WEB-SLINGING WALL-CRAWLER!*

FACE IT TIGER, YOU JUST HIT THE JACKPOT!

I SAID FACE IT TIGER, YOU JUST--
SIT DOWN!

UNFORTUNATELY, DAILY BUGLE PUBLISHER AND LONGTIME A-HOLE J. JONAH JAMESON COULDN'T BE HERE TODAY, SO HE SENT A SPIDER SLAYER IN HIS STEAD.
SPIDER SLAYER...?

IT SEEMED TO ME, YOU LIVED YOUR LIFE, LIKE A CANDLE IN THE WIND...
NEVER KNOWING WHO TO CLING TO, WHEN THE RAIN-
BZZZT
KILL ALL HUMANS!
THAT'S NOT HOW IT GOES.

WOW, ROBOTS ARE NO FUN.
ONLY THE MALE ONES.
HEY, WHERE IS JONAH ANYWAY?

AT THE DAILY BUGLE...
EH? CHICKS CAN VOTE NOW?
GUESS I'VE BEEN TOO WRAPPED UP WITH SPIDER-MAN TO RUN THESE OTHER STORIES.
AH WELL, DO WHAT YOU KNOW BEST, I SAY.
REJECTED
MAN WALKS ON MOON
REJECTED
WOMEN TO VOTE!

SPIDER-MAN WAS LIKE A FAMILY MEMBER. I CAN STILL REMEMBER WHEN I FELL IN LOVE WITH HIM AS A CHARACTER: IT WAS WHEN MARVEL BACKED UP THAT FIRST GARBAGE TRUCK FULL OF CASH AND EMPTIED IT INTO MY NEW IN-GROUND POOL (THAT'S JUST A LITTLE JOKE THERE; I DON'T HAVE AN IN-GROUND POOL).

SPEAKING OF MILLAR, WHATEVER THAT MIME DID TO HIM BACK IN THE '70S SURE SOURED HIM ON CLOWNS. I REMEMBER ONE TIME WE WERE TAKING THE CHUNNEL BACK FROM ENGLAND AND THIS BIRTHDAY RENT-A-CLOWN ASKED IF A SEAT OPPOSITE US WAS TAKEN. I NEVER KNEW THE HUMAN BODY HAD THAT MUCH BLOOD (WHICH I LATER USED AS REFERENCE IN MY 'TORSO' GRAPHIC NOVEL, AVAILABLE FOR $24.95 ON JINXWORLD.COM). HEY, DID YOU KNOW MICHAEL AVON OEMING'S A DUDE? FOR THE FIRST THREE YEARS WE WERE WORKING TOGETHER I THOUGH HE WAS A CHICK. GO FIGURE.

AND HEY, ALL YOU PEOPLE BUYING 'ULTIMATE SPIDEY' BETTER GET IN LINE AND START BUYING 'THE PULSE.' I KNOW, I KNOW... IT DOESN'T HAVE F-WORDS IN IT ANYMORE, BUT NOW IT'S GOT NORMAN OSBORN STRANGLING SECRETARIES AND DUMPING THEIR BODIES IN THE HUDSON! AWESOME, RIGHT? BOY, THERE'S NOTHING LIKE STRANGLING SOMEONE AND WATCHING THE LIGHT FADE FROM THEIR EYES. OR SO GARTH ENNIS TELLS ME. SPEAKING OF WHICH, WHEN'S THE LAST TIME ANYONE SAW GLENN FABRY? TEN BUCKS SAYS HE BEAT ENNIS ONE TOO MANY TIMES IN 'MARIO KART' OR SOMETHING.

MEANWHILE, AT THE POSH OFFICES OF THE AMAZING FRIENDS...
THIS RESUME, WHILE MOIST, IS FANTASTIC!
YOU'RE OUR REPLACEMENT MEMBER!

WELCOME ABOARD, SWAMP THING!
AS YOU CAN TELL, SPIDER-MAN'S DEATH HAS US ALL A LITTLE SCARED AND—
SSSSSS...

FOOMP!

OH, MY HAIR!
I REALLY AM MISS ANGELICA JINX!*
*WINNER, MOST OBSCURE JOKE, 2004.

GREETINGS, I'M ALAN MOORE. ONCE AGAIN, THERE SEEMS TO BE SOME CONFUSION. THE MOSSY GENTLEMAN FROM THE PREVIOUS EXCHANGE IS MAN-THING, NOT SWAMP THING.

MAN-THING'S TOUCH BURNS THOSE WHO KNOW FEAR, WHILE SWAMP THING'S TOUCH IS MERELY INAPPROPRIATE.
AND THIS IS SOME GOOD FREAKIN' HAM!
THIS ISN'T FAT... IT'S MUSCLE!

EVEN THOUGH WE HAD OUR DIFFERENCES, I'LL ALWAYS FONDLY REMEMBER MY RELATIONSHIP WITH SPIDER-MAN.
ESPECIALLY THE TIME HE SLIPPED ME A TWENTY TO OFF THAT ANNOYING BLOND GIRLFRIEND HE—

WHOOSH!
KUNG-FU DODGE!

HA!
MISSED ME THAT TIME, YOU STUPID GLIDER!
SAW IT COMING.
HEY, HE OWED ME $20!
SO LONG, SUCKERSSSSS...

WHO THE...PAUL REUBENS!?!
I'M THE JACKAL! I WAS SPIDER-MAN'S PROFESSOR IN COLLEGE.

I WAS SO FOND OF THE BOY I CLONED HIM AND LITTERED THE ENTIRE MARVEL UNIVERSE WITH 'EM.
THERE'S ONE NOW.

BUT...BUT WHY DID YOU LET EVERYONE THINK YOU WERE DEAD?
TAX PURPOSES. AND HAVE YOU TRIED THE HAM?
END

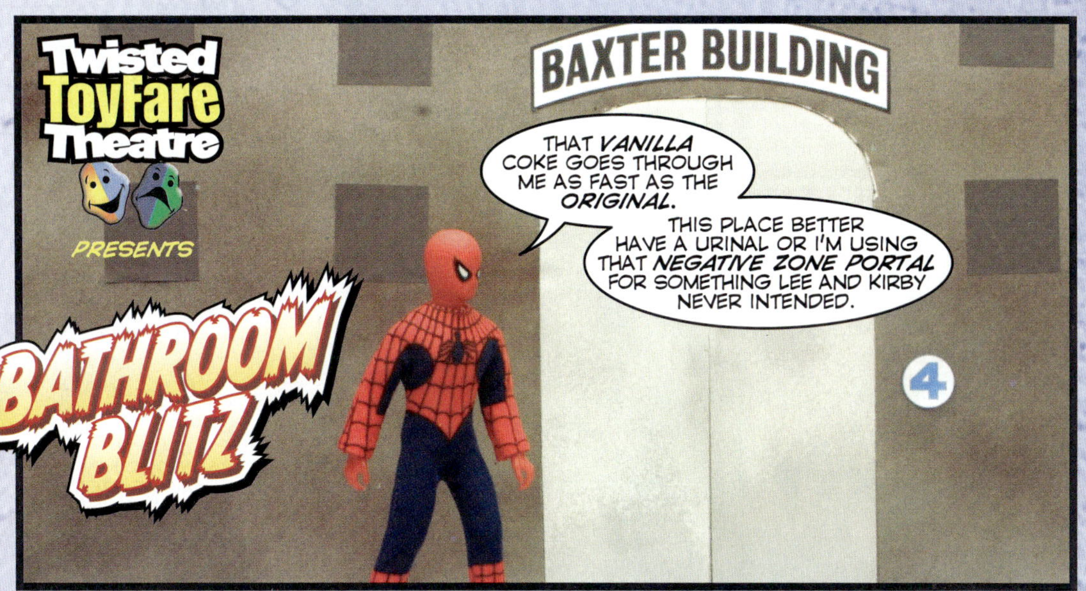
Twisted ToyFare Theatre
PRESENTS
BATHROOM BLITZ
BAXTER BUILDING
THAT VANILLA COKE GOES THROUGH ME AS FAST AS THE ORIGINAL.
THIS PLACE BETTER HAVE A URINAL OR I'M USING THAT NEGATIVE ZONE PORTAL FOR SOMETHING LEE AND KIRBY NEVER INTENDED.
4

WHAT? SPIDER-MAN BREAKING INTO THE BAXTER BUILDING? YOU MUST BE TRYING TO PROVE YOURSELF TO JOIN THE TEAM.
THAT SETTLES IT! WELCOME TO THE FANTASTIC FOUR!
I WONDER IF THE URINAL CAKES HAVE LITTLE 4'S ON 'EM...

UH, ACTUALLY, I WAS JUST...
UNFORTUNATLY, SINCE ALL THE MERCHANDISE SAYS '4', ONE OF US MUST GO.
SORRY, BEN OLD CHUM.
YOU CAN'T FIRE ME, STRETCHO... I'M JEWISH!

"THAT'S TRUE, BEN. I DON'T WANT AL SHARPTON BREATHING DOWN MY NECK. SUE, YOU'RE FIRED."
I GOT TWO REASONS RIGHT HERE WHY FIRING ME IS BAD FOR SALES.

"GOOD POINT...ER, POINTS. JOHNNY...?"
YOU CAN'T FIRE ME...I'M A WAR HERO!
I FOUGHT VALIANTLY ALONGSIDE CAPTAIN AMERICA AND THE INVADERS IN WORLD WAR II!
SUCKER.

BUT IF I CAN'T FIRE BEN, SUE, OR JOHNNY, THAT MEANS...THAT MEANS IT'S GOTTA BE...

...ME.
YOINK!
RRRRRIP!

...WISH I WAS JEWISH...
GREETINGS, EARTHLINGS! I, THE SILVER SURFER, BRING TIDINGS OF BIG AKIRA-LIKE EXPLOSIONS FROM MY MASTER GALACTUS, DEVOURER OF WORLDS!
WHO?
OH NO! ONLY OUR NEW TEAM LEADER CAN SAVE US! WHAT DO WE DO, SPIDER-MAN?

SPIDER-MAN...?

FLUSH!
YOU'RE OUT OF TP.
AND GOOD LUCK WITH THAT GALACTUS THING. I'M OUTTIE.

I HUNGER...
ALL RIGHT, BIG GUY... THEY'VE BEEN WARNED-- SO CHOW DOWN!
AW, CRAP...

DAILY BUGLE
NEW YORK'S FINEST DAILY NEWSPAPER
FINAL
GALACTUS EATS EARTH!
Where Is This Being Printed?!?
DEAD SPIDER-MAN STILL A MENACE TO DEAD COPS!
END

THE BEST OF BIG SHOTS

For many people, *ToyFare* means two things—"TTT" and Big Shots. Big Shots were single-panel gags found throughout the price guide, ensuring an entertaining counter-balance to cold, hard numbers. Eventually we decided that they seemed redundant and did away with them, but fans still ask to see them again. So here they are, collected for the first time ever—the very best of Big Shots.

ToyFare Spring Special (Sept. 1997)

ToyFare #1 (September, 1997)

ToyFare #2 (October, 1997)

ToyFare #4 (December, 1997)

ToyFare #4 (December, 1997)

ToyFare #17 (January, 1999)

PHOTOS: PAUL SCHIRALDI

ToyFare #17 (January, 1999)

ToyFare #19 (March, 1999)

ToyFare #20 (April, 1999)

ToyFare #23 (July, 1999)

PHOTOS: PAUL SCHIRALDI

ToyFare #26 (October, 1999)

ToyFare #26 (October, 1999)

ToyFare #27 (November, 1999)

ToyFare #27 (November, 1999)

ToyFare #28 (December, 1999)

ToyFare #31 (March, 2000)

ToyFare #32 (April, 2000)

ToyFare #32 (April, 2000)

PHOTOS: PAUL SCHIRALDI

ToyFare #33 (May, 2000)

ToyFare #37 (September, 2000)

ToyFare #37 (September, 2000)

ToyFare #37 (September, 2000)

PHOTOS: PAUL SCHIRALDI

ToyFare #46 (June, 2001)

ToyFare #46 (June, 2001)

ToyFare #47 (July, 2001)

ToyFare #49 (September, 2001)

ToyFare #57 (May, 2002)

ToyFare #57 (May, 2002)

ToyFare #57 (May, 2002)

ToyFare #61 (September, 2002)

MATRIX, GUMBY & SHAFT PHOTOS: PAUL SCHIRALDI

ToyFare **#61** (September, 2002)

ToyFare **#63** (November, 2002)

ToyFare **#67** (March, 2003)

ToyFare **#71** (July, 2003)

ToyFare **#81** (May, 2004)

ToyFare **#83** (July, 2004)

WELCOME TO THE

A 'TTT' LOVER'S GUIDE TO THE HOME OF

MASTER BATHROOM

The only bathroom with a shower, it has been used by more people than Spidey likes. Besides occasionally finding one of Thor's tub toys, Spidey has had to contend with Cobra troopers flushing the toilet and making the water turn red-hot.

MASTER BEDROOM

Spidey doesn't like people coming into his bedroom, so he keeps the door shut most of the time. However, that hasn't kept Morpheus, Dr. Strange and a host of others from coming in through the window.

DOWNSTAIRS BATHROOM

The bathroom most often used by guests, it's been pretty much a no-man's land ever since Man-Thing took a dump in it during a party.

COBRA BASE

Some people have mice. Spidey has Cobras. Building an elaborate network of hangars and barracks, Cobra has turned Spidey's house into the ultimate suburban fortress.

DOLLHOUSE

MEGO SPIDEY By the *ToyFare* Staff

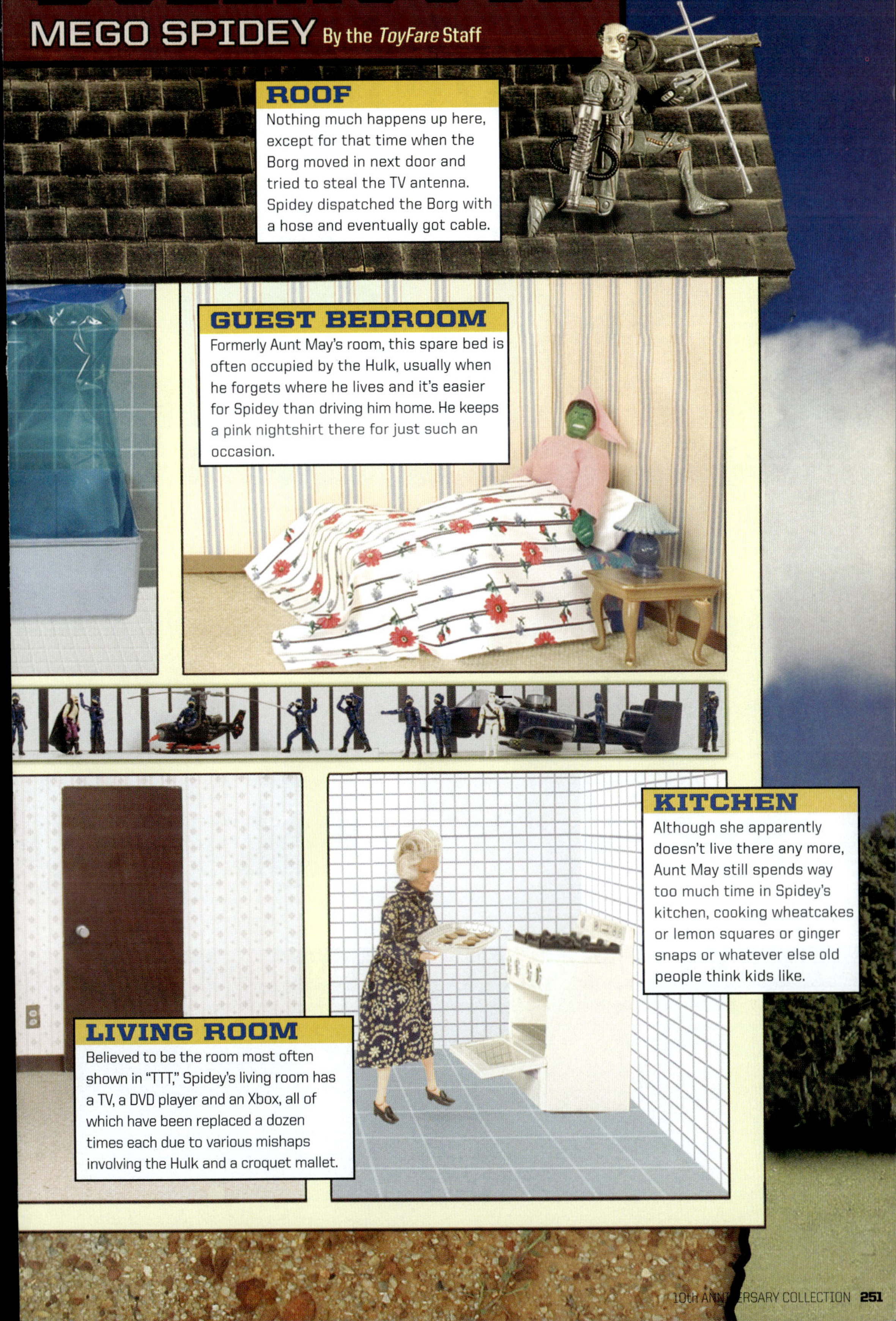

ROOF

Nothing much happens up here, except for that time when the Borg moved in next door and tried to steal the TV antenna. Spidey dispatched the Borg with a hose and eventually got cable.

GUEST BEDROOM

Formerly Aunt May's room, this spare bed is often occupied by the Hulk, usually when he forgets where he lives and it's easier for Spidey than driving him home. He keeps a pink nightshirt there for just such an occasion.

KITCHEN

Although she apparently doesn't live there any more, Aunt May still spends way too much time in Spidey's kitchen, cooking wheatcakes or lemon squares or ginger snaps or whatever else old people think kids like.

LIVING ROOM

Believed to be the room most often shown in "TTT," Spidey's living room has a TV, a DVD player and an Xbox, all of which have been replaced a dozen times each due to various mishaps involving the Hulk and a croquet mallet.

STRANGE CUSTOMS

OUR TEN FAVORITE CUSTOM-MADE MEGO FIGURES FROM THE HISTORY OF 'TTT'

1. DR. DOOM

By Charlee Flatt

Debuting in the first full-length strip in issue #1 (see page 67), Doom quickly established himself as a fountain of impotent rage and has been a staff favorite ever since, mostly due to his amazing poseability, the tailoring of his tunic and the expression of burning hatred on his face.

2. CYCLOPS

By Charlee Flatt

Cyclops first debuted in *ToyFare* #21 ("House Party," see page 97), where his wide-open mouth and penchant for expository dialogue proved themselves to be a wondrous combination. Dull as toast to read about, he would be told to shut up by Prof. X repeatedly.

3. RED SKULL

By John Dunivant

Actually the second Skull we've had created, this one replaced the Flatt original in the post-Crisis *ToyFare* #1 TTT strip. His pupils are painted so that he can appear deadly serious or like he's rolling his eyes, which allows us to play him as menacing, exasperated or both.

4. MAN-WOLF

By Vince Callaghan

We had the always-reliable Callaghan craft this figure specifically for the "Walk Like a Man-Wolf" strip (*ToyFare* #104). The head conveys equal parts ferocity and innocent excitement, and it makes us laugh just by looking at it.

5. SHE-HULK

By Bret Bolden

We don't know how Bret Bolden did it, but She-Hulk's got real hair, a unique face sculpt and a form-fitting outfit—all challenging orders. Then we dressed her in an unflattering business suit her first time out of the gate (*ToyFare* #91, see page 149). Oh, well.

Ah, Megos. Not only are you a source of nostalgia for toy collectors in their 30s and 40s, you're also damn hilarious. Sadly, there aren't very many of you. All in all, there are fewer than 25 actual Mego dolls that the "Twisted ToyFare" photographers use on a regular basis, and only 11 of those are fan-favorite Marvel Comics characters. So how do we fill out our cast of Marvel superheroes and villains? We make 'em! Talented customizers have swelled our Mego ranks over the years, and these are ten of our favorites.

6. ELECTRO

By Vince Callaghan

Amongst all the "TTT" customs in heavy rotation, Electro, with his spiky starfish mask, seemed the ripest for breakage, but he's proven surprisingly resilient, even when he's being put in crazy dance poses worthy of Honey Daniels (*ToyFare* #81).

7. BUCKY

By Tom Key and Kris Meadows

While Tom and Kris only made one figure for us, it's one that we use a lot. However, every time we start to learn a little bit about him he gets killed. We give him shocked, scared or dead eyes so often that we hardly ever see his real ones! (They're blue.)

8. TARANTULA

By Vince Callaghan

The only way this Spider-Man villain could be any more like his comic book version would be if the spikes on his shoes were razor sharp—thankfully, Vince blunted the points on this Spanish stereotype's felonious footwear, saving us money on Band-Aids.

9. LEADER

By Vince Callaghan

Well, look at the big brain on Leader! When choosing which incarnation of the Leader we wanted Vince to make, we went with "tall head" over "bulging brain"—funny rather than creepy. Still, he manages to convey a sense of smug superiority in all of his endeavors.

10. MAN-THING

By Nick Robinson

There's something inhumanly soulless about Man-Thing, but there's a sadness about him as well, which is why he's treated like a harmless deer by other characters, despite his ability to set you on fire with a touch (as he did to Franklin Richards in *ToyFare* #38).

ROAD RAGE

OUR ILLUSTRATED MAP TO THE CITY OF MEGOVILLE

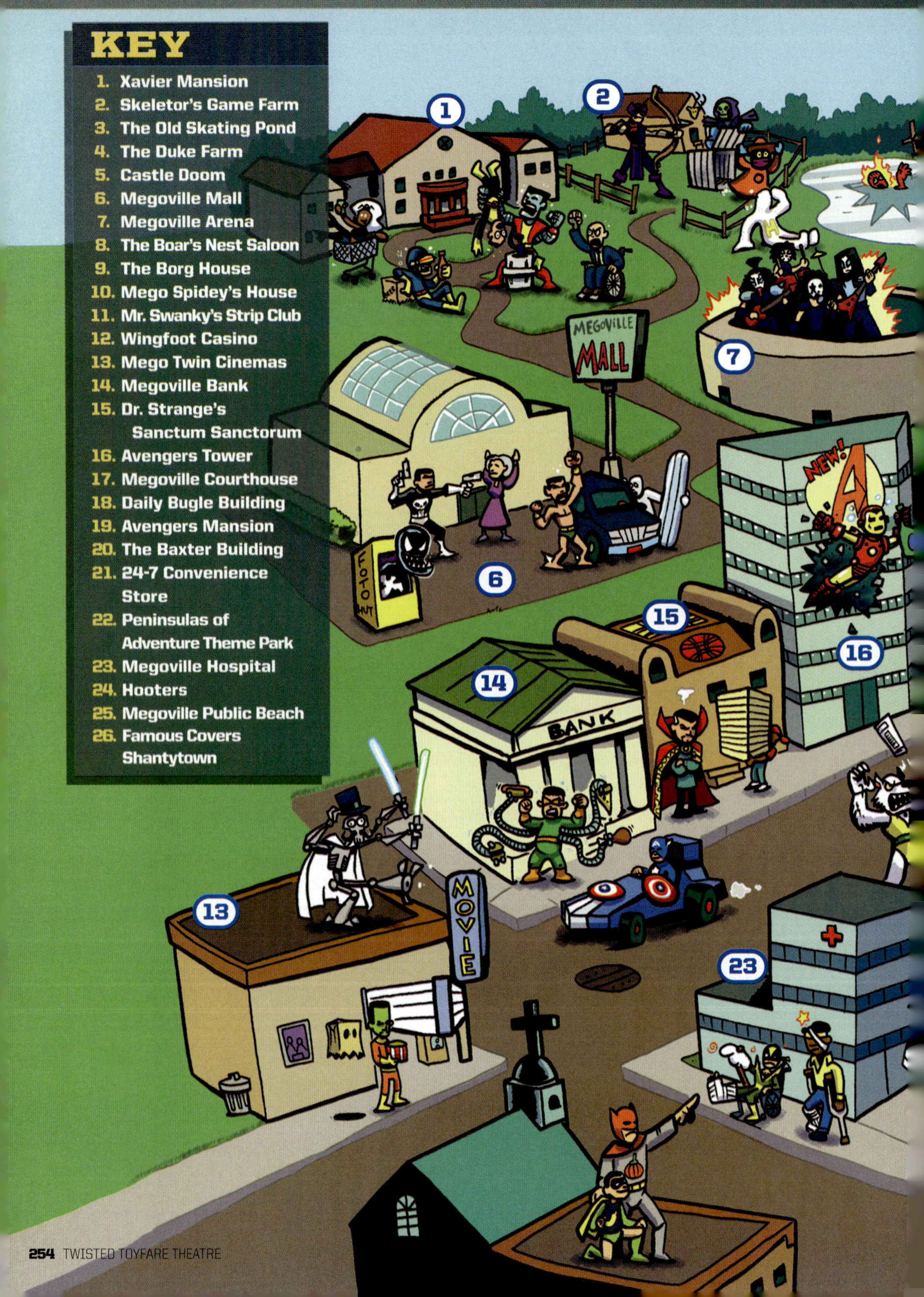

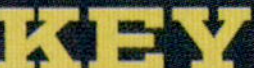

KEY
1. Xavier Mansion
2. Skeletor's Game Farm
3. The Old Skating Pond
4. The Duke Farm
5. Castle Doom
6. Megoville Mall
7. Megoville Arena
8. The Boar's Nest Saloon
9. The Borg House
10. Mego Spidey's House
11. Mr. Swanky's Strip Club
12. Wingfoot Casino
13. Mego Twin Cinemas
14. Megoville Bank
15. Dr. Strange's Sanctum Sanctorum
16. Avengers Tower
17. Megoville Courthouse
18. Daily Bugle Building
19. Avengers Mansion
20. The Baxter Building
21. 24-7 Convenience Store
22. Peninsulas of Adventure Theme Park
23. Megoville Hospital
24. Hooters
25. Megoville Public Beach
26. Famous Covers Shantytown
MEGOVILLE MALL
NEW!
FOTO HUT
BANK
MOVIE

We realize that after 120 strips, it's hard to keep track of where everything is in Megoville. Is Castle Doom near Spidey's house? Is Hooters near the strip club? Wait, isn't Castle Doom in Latveria? Well, to help you keep everything straight, we created this handy-dandy map so you can pinpoint the action as it happens!

ILLUSTRATION BY RYAN DUNLAVEY

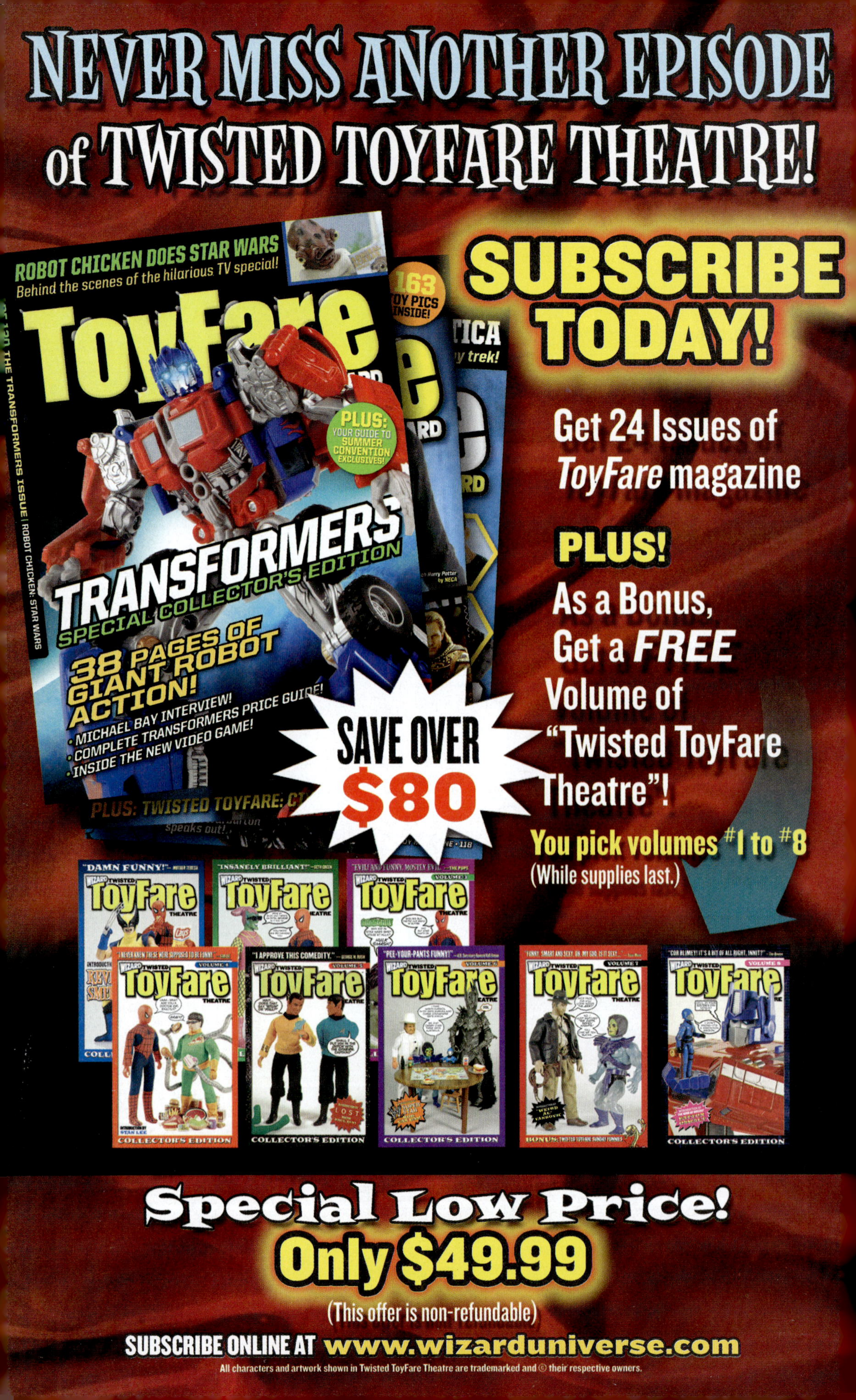